INTERACTIVE COMPUTING

SOFTWARE SKILLS

Microsoft®
Excel 97

Kenneth C. Laudon
Azimuth Multimedia Productions, Inc

Evan Kantor

Michael Banino

Erica Laudon

 **Irwin
McGraw-Hill**

Boston   Burr Ridge, IL   Dubuque, IA   Madison, WI   New York   San Francisco   St. Louis
Bangkok   Bogotá   Caracas   Lisbon   London   Madrid
Mexico City   Milan   New Delhi   Seoul   Singapore   Sydney   Taipei   Toronto

Irwin/McGraw-Hill

A Division of The McGraw-Hill Companies

Interactive Computing Software Skills
Microsoft® Excel 97

Copyright © 1998, by The McGraw-Hill Companies, Inc. All rights reserved. Printed in the United States of America. Except as permitted under the United States Copyright Act of 1976, no part of this publication may be reproduced or distributed in any form or by any means, or stored in a data base or retrieval system, without the prior written permission of the publisher.

This book is printed on acid-free paper.

3 4 5 6 7 8 9 0 CRS CRS 3 2 1 0 9

ISBN 0-07-038443-6

Editorial director: *Michael Junior*
Sponsoring editor: *Rhonda Sands*
Marketing manager: *James Rogers*
Project manager: *Richard DeVitto*
Cover designer: *Amanda Kavanagh*
Interior design: *Yvonne Quirk*
Development: *Jane Laudon*
Editorial Assistant: *Kenneth Rosenblatt*
Layout: *Evan Kantor, Michael Banino*
Compositor: *Pat Rogondino*
Printer: *Courier Stoughton*

Library of Congress Cataloging-in-Publication Data

Interactive computing software skills : Microsoft Excel 97 / Kenneth C.
  Laudon ... [et al.]
    p.   cm.
    Includes index.
    ISBN 0-07-038443-6
    1. Microsoft Excel for Windows. 2. Business--Computer programs.
  3. Electronic spreadsheets. I. Laudon, Kenneth C., 1944-
  HF5548.4.M523I58 1998
  005.369--dc21   97-46810
                                                          CIP

http://www.mhhe.com

Contents

Contents (continued)

Preface

Interactive Computing:
Software Skills
Microsoft Office 97

· ·

The *Interactive Computing: Software Skills* series provides you with an illustrated interactive environment for learning introductory software skills using Microsoft Office 97. The Interactive Computing Series is composed of both illustrated books and multimedia interactive CD-ROMs for Windows 95 and each Office 97 program: Word 97, Excel 97, Access 97, and PowerPoint 97.

The books and the CD-ROMs are closely coordinated. The coverage of basic skills is the same in CDs and books, although the books go into more advanced skill areas. Because of their close coordination, the books and CD-ROMs can be used together very effectively, or they can each be used as stand-alone learning tools. The multimedia interactive CD-ROMs get you started very quickly on basic and intermediate skills. The books cover this material and then go farther.

It's up to you. You can choose how you want to learn. In either case the Interactive Computing Series gives you the easiest and most powerful way to learn Microsoft Office 97.

Skills, Concepts, and Steps

In both the book and the CD-ROM, each lesson is organized around *skills*, *concepts*, and *steps*. Each lesson is divided into a number of skills. The basic concept of each skill is first explained, including where that skill is used in practical work situations. The concept is then followed by a series of concise instructions or steps that the student follows to learn the skill. A *running case study* throughout reinforces the skill by giving a real-world focus to the learning process.

The Learning Approach

We have taken a highly graphical and multimedia approach to learning. Text, screen shots, graphics, and on the CD-ROM, voice, video, and digital world simulation are all used to teach concepts and skills. The result is a powerful learning package.

Using the Book

In the book, each skill is described in a two-page graphical spread (Figure 1). The left side of the two-page spread describes the skill, the concept, and the steps needed to perform the skill. The right side of the spread uses screen shots to show you how the screen should look at key stages.

Figure 1

Skill: Each lesson is divided into a number of specific skills.

Concept: A concise description of *why* the skill is useful and where it is commonly used.

Running case: A real-world case ties the skill and concept to a practical situation.

Do It!: Step-by-step directions show you how to use the skill.

Skill   Examining the Windows Explorer

Concept

The **Windows Explorer**, found in the Programs menu on the Start menu, is similar to My Computer. Both are file management tools that allow you to view the contents of your computer. The Windows Explorer is more powerful and provides you with more options than My Computer. The Windows Explorer displays itself as the two-paneled window you see in Figure 2-4, allowing you to work with more than one drive, file, or folder at a time. The left panel shows all the folders and disk drives on your computer. The right panel is a display of the contents of a selected folder or drive. This two-paneled window creates a more detailed view of a specific folder and makes for easier file manipulation, especially copying and moving.

Do It!

Mike wrote a letter to his mother but forgot where he put it. He uses the Windows Explorer to find the file.

1. Click the **Start** button, highlight the **Programs** menu, and click **Windows Explorer** to open the Windows Explorer window.

2. If the toolbar is not already showing, click the **View** menu and select the **Toolbar** command.

3. Click the **Up One Level** button 🔼 until you get to the top of the hierarchy. When you are at the top, **Desktop** will appear in the **Go to a different folder** list box, and the Up One Level button will be dimmed.

4. The list of items you see in the left panel will differ from computer to computer depending on the applications and files that are installed. Click the small ➕ next to the My Computer icon to reveal its contents. A ➕ next to an icon indicates that the item can be expanded to display other folders that are contained in that drive or folder. There will be no ➕ if the folder only contains files. Expanding an icon reveals another level of the hierarchy. (Clicking the ➖ collapses a drive or folder's contents back into the parent drive or folder.) The folder in the left, All Folders, panel, which is selected, appears opened.

5. Ask your professor where the student files are located. If they are on a student disk, insert that floppy disk into your computer's (A:) disk drive.

6. Click the ➕ for the 3½ **Floppy** drive icon, or click the icon for the drive where the student files are located if they are already stored on your computer or over a network. The folder named Mike's Folder will be shown under the icon for the disk where your student files are stored.

7. Click the ➕ next to **Mike's Folder** to expand it. Then click the folder titled **Personal**. The contents of the Personal folder will be displayed in the right panel.

8. To see what is in the **Letters** folder, double-click the folder's icon. **Letter to Mom** and **Letter to Amanda** are here.

9. Close the Windows Explorer by pressing the [**Alt**] and [**F4**] keys.

32

End-of-Lesson Features

In the book, the learning in each lesson is reinforced at the end by a quiz and a skills review called Interactivity, which provides a step-by-step exercise and a real-world problem to solve independently.

Figure 1 (continued)

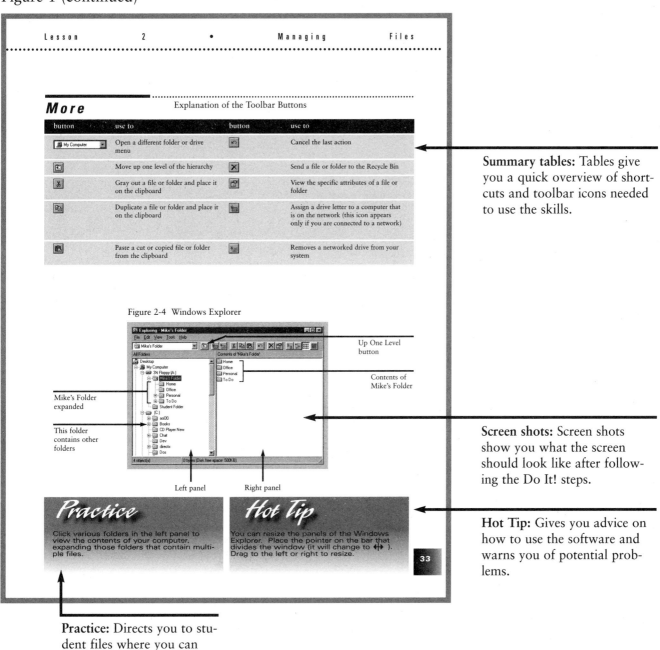

Summary tables: Tables give you a quick overview of short-cuts and toolbar icons needed to use the skills.

Screen shots: Screen shots show you what the screen should look like after following the Do It! steps.

Hot Tip: Gives you advice on how to use the software and warns you of potential problems.

Practice: Directs you to student files where you can practice this skill.

Using the Interactive CD-ROM

The Interactive Computing multimedia CD-ROM provides an unparalleled learning environment in which you can learn software skills faster and better than in books alone. The CD-
ROM provides a unique interactive environment in which you can learn to use software faster
and remember it better. The CD-ROM uses the same lessons, skills, concepts, and Do It! steps
as found in the book, but presents the material using voice, video, animation, and precise simulation of the software you are learning. A typical CD-ROM contents screen shows the major
elements of a lesson (Figure 2).

Skills list: A list of skills
permits you to jump
directly to any skill you
want to learn or review.

Figure 2

Lessons and skills: The lessons
and skills covered in the CD are
closely coordinated with those of
the book.

Interactive sessions: The skills
you learn are immediately tested
in interactive sessions with the
TeacherWizard.

Review: At the end of each lesson
is a review of all the concepts
covered, as well as review questions.

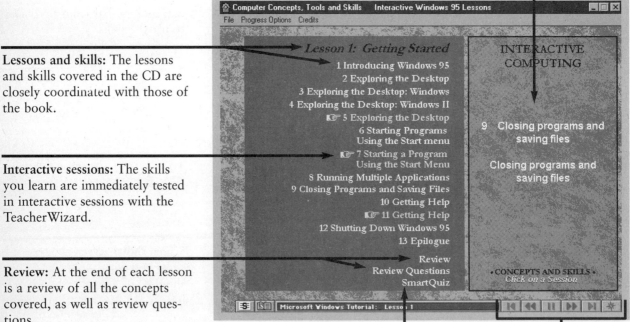

SmartQuiz: Each lesson has
a SmartQuiz that tests your
ability to accomplish tasks
within a simulated software
environment.

User controls: Precise
and simple user controls
permit you to start, stop,
pause, jump forward or
backward a sentence, or
jump forward or back-
ward an entire skill. A
single Navigation Star
takes you back to the lesson's table of contents.

Unique Features of the CD-ROM: TeacherWizards™ and SmartQuiz™

Interactive Computing: Software Skills offers many leading-edge features of the CD-ROM currently found in no other learning product on the market. One such feature is *interactive exercises* in which you are asked to demonstrate your command of a software skill in a precisely simulated software environment. Your actions are closely followed by a digital TeacherWizard that guides you with additional information if you make a mistake. When you correctly complete the action called for by the TeacherWizard, you are congratulated and prompted to continue the lesson. If you make a mistake, the TeacherWizard gently lets you know: "No, that's not the right icon. Click on the Open File icon at the left side of the toolbar on top of the screen." No matter how many mistakes you make, the TeacherWizard is there to help you.

Another leading-edge feature is the end-of-lesson SmartQuiz. Unlike the multiple choice and matching questions found in the book quiz, the SmartQuiz puts you in a simulated digital software world and asks you to show your mastery of skills while actually working with the software (Figure 3).

Figure 3

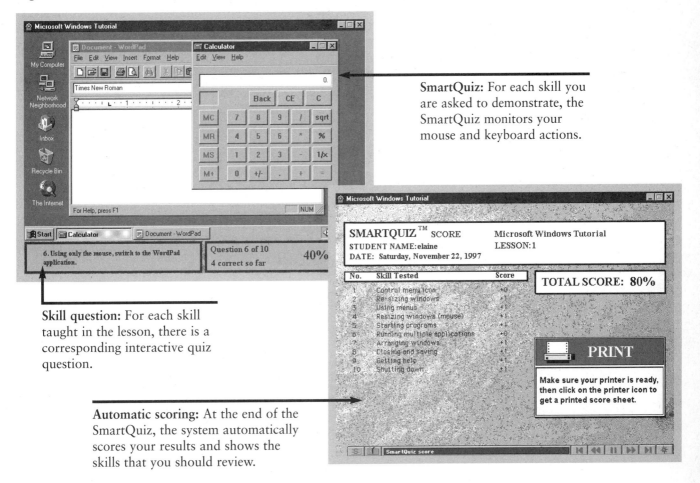

SmartQuiz: For each skill you are asked to demonstrate, the SmartQuiz monitors your mouse and keyboard actions.

Skill question: For each skill taught in the lesson, there is a corresponding interactive quiz question.

Automatic scoring: At the end of the SmartQuiz, the system automatically scores your results and shows the skills that you should review.

Using the CD-ROM and the Book Together

The CD-ROM and the book are designed to support each another. There is a close correspondence between the lessons and skills taught in the book and the CD for introductory levels of the software (Lessons 1 through 4), as well as between the case study used in the CDs and the books. Generally, the books have more lessons and go farther into advanced topics than the CD does, while the CD-ROM demonstrates the basic steps in more detail. Here are tips on using the CD and accompanying book together:

- You can use the book and the CD together at your student lab workstation or at home. Place them side by side and follow along in both at the same time.

- You can use the book when you do not have access to a computer, and use the CD by itself at school or at home.

- You can use the CD first to gain a quick understanding of the software, then use the book later at home or school ro review and deepen your understanding.

Student Files

The *Interactive Computing: Software Skills* books require that students have access to accompanying student files for the practice and test sessions. The instructor and students using the texts in class are granted the right to post the student files on any network or stand-alone computer, or to distribute the files on individual diskettes. You can download the student files from the Interactive Computing Web site at **http://www.mhhe.com/cit/apps/laudon/**, or request them through your Irwin/McGraw-Hill representative.

Supplementary Learning and Teaching Tools

The Student Center at http://www.mhhe.com/cit/apps/laudon/ provides the following supporting information:

- Web exercises: These exercises can be assigned by your instructor. Or you can try them on your own. Your instructor has the solutions.

- Cool sites: Web news, new technology, Web opportunities, entertainment.

- Message board: Talk to other students who are using the series.

- Multimedia action: Cool demos.

- Course help: Choose the course you're enrolled in. Then choose exercises, multimedia demos, free software, or course information.

The Faculty Lounge at http://www.mhhe.com/cit/apps/laudon/ provides the following instructional support:

- Exercises and solutions

- Teaching strategies

- Instructor message board

- Multimedia action

- Cool Web site

- Course help

Local Area Network Testing Facility

McGraw-Hill and Azimuth Multimedia have designed and produced a revolutionary and unique Network Testing Facility™ (NTF) that tests acquired software skills in a safe, simulated software environment. Operating on a network, the NTF permits students to take a self-paced exam from their workstations at home, at school, or in the classroom. The NTF automatically tracks student scores, and allows the instructor to build screens that indicate an individual student's progress or which skills may need more emphasis for the entire class.

Contact your McGraw-Hill representative for further information on the NTF.

Acknowledgments

The Interactive Computing Series is a cooperative effort of many individuals, each contributing to a team effort. Our goal is to provide students and instructors with the most powerful and enjoyable learning environment using both traditional text and new multimedia techniques. Achieving this goal requires the contributions of text authors, multimedia screenplay writers, multimedia designers, animators, graphic artists, editors, computer scientists, and student testers.

Our special thanks to Frank Ruggirello, who envisioned and initiated the Interactive Computing Series. Peter Jovanovich and Gary Burke of McGraw-Hill management generously supported a technological leap into the future of teaching and learning. Rhonda Sands, our editor, has gently pushed us to higher levels of performance and encouraged us to do the best we can.

L E S S O N

1

INTRODUCTION TO SPREADSHEET SOFTWARE

Microsoft Excel is a computer application that improves your ability to record data and then extract results from it. With Excel, you can enter text labels and numerical values into an electronic spreadsheet, a grid made up of columns and rows. The computerized worksheets you work with in Excel resemble handwritten ledgers, with which you may already be familiar. Being able to use spreadsheet software can help you both professionally and personally. By providing an organized structure to work in, Excel can increase the efficiency with which you conduct business and track your own affairs. Excel's ability to perform and automate calculations saves time and decreases the possibility of error.

Using Excel, you will learn how to create a spreadsheet employing proper design techniques. You will then explore the application and become familiar with its basic elements and operations. Later on, some of Excel's more advanced features such as formulas, what-if analysis, and macros will broaden your knowledge of how to create and work with a spreadsheet. If you need assistance while using Excel, the program includes an extensive help facility, as well as the ability to access online support via the World Wide Web.

Case Study:
Kay Samoy is the owner of a small but successful company that distributes a wide variety of dog accessories such as treats, furnishings, and toys. She would like to use Excel to track her income, expenses, and profits electronically now that her business is growing. Kay will begin by familiarizing herself with the application. Then she will take the first steps toward creating an effective spreadsheet.

Introducing Excel

Concept

Microsoft Excel is an electronic spreadsheet application designed to make the creation and use of professional quality spreadsheets fast and easy. A **spreadsheet** is a table composed of rows and columns that store text and numbers for easy viewing and tabulation. Electronic spreadsheets are very useful for performing rapid and accurate calculations on groups of interrelated numbers.

Using Excel, you can:

- Organize information rapidly and accurately. With the proper data and formulas Excel automatically calculates your results. With a paper and pencil spreadsheet, you would have to do all of the calculations manually.

- Recalculate automatically. Fixing errors in Excel is easy. When you find a mistake and correct the entry, Excel automatically recalculates all related data.

- Keep track of the effect that changing one piece of data has on related numbers. You can postulate changes that may occur in the future and see how they could change the results of your calculations. This powerful decision-making feature is called "what-if" analysis.

- Display data as graphs or charts. Excel allows you to display numeric data graphically in the form of charts, which are automatically updated as the data changes. For example, Figure 1-1 shows the data in a spreadsheet for income and expenditures that can also be displayed in the form of a pie chart. Charts often make relationships among data easier to understand.

More

Microsoft Excel stores each **workbook** you create as an individual document in the computer's memory. A document, also called a file, can be a single worksheet or may contain many of pages of data and graphs. Each file should be given a unique name so it can be easily differentiated from other files. Excel documents are given the file extension .xls. A **file extension** is a three letter code, separated from the file name with a period, called a dot, that tells the computer what application is associated with a particular file.

Figure 1-1 A worksheet made with Microsoft Excel

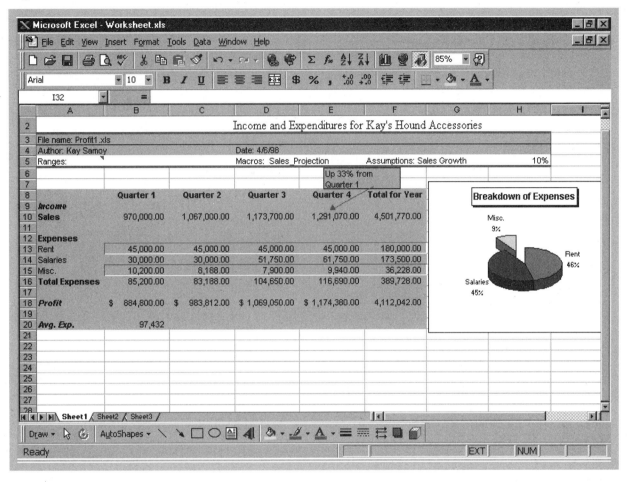

Hot Tip

An electronic spreadsheet application, such as Excel, allows you to easily share data between worksheets or other applications so that it need not be entered again.

Designing a Worksheet

Concept

The organization of the spreadsheet is shaped by its goal or purpose. By carefully planning and designing your spreadsheet, you can make your work more accurate and easily understood. A well-designed spreadsheet has four sections: documentation, assumptions, input, and results. These sections are illustrated in Figure 1-2.

- The first section contains **documentation**, consisting of a complete description of the name of the author, the purpose of the spreadsheet, the date it was created, and the name of the spreadsheet file. Documentation should also specify location of any cell ranges and macros. Ranges are blocks of columns and rows that are useful for performing certain types of calculations and for displaying data. Macros are instructions for automating spreadsheet tasks. We discuss ranges in Lesson 3 and macros in Lesson 5.

- The second section of a spreadsheet is used to display **assumptions**. Assumptions are variable factors that may change in a worksheet. For example, Kay's profit projections assume that sales will expand by 10% each quarter. When her sales numbers are changed, they will affect the amount of profit. It is easier to change documented assumptions than undocumented ones. Assumptions are useful when conducting "what-if" analysis based on calculating the effect of changes in spreadsheet data. For instance, what if sales only grow by 5%? You will learn more about what-if analysis in Lesson 2.

- The third section of the spreadsheet stores **input**, the numbers that you are working with. In Figure 1-2, the input section contains data for income and expenditures. Input data is generally arranged in blocks of numbers organized in columns and rows.

- The fourth section is a **results**, or output, section, which displays the results of the calculations made on the input data. Output data is generally placed below and to the right of input data.

More

When designing a spreadsheet it is important to think about whether or not you will be using **macros**. Macros are used in worksheets and many other applications to simplify repetitive or complicated tasks. You can record a series of actions that you perform in Excel as a macro, then play back the macro by choosing its name from the appropriate dialog box. Macros can save time and improve quality because they perform a series of commands the same way each time. You will learn how to create and use macros in Lesson 5.

Figure 1-2 Organization of a well-designed spreadsheet

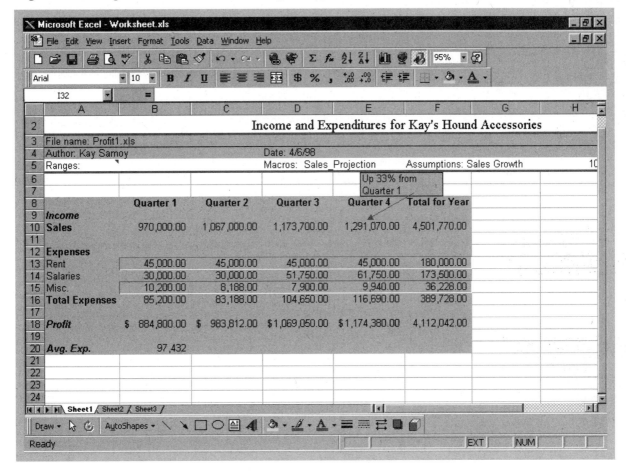

Hot Tip

It is a good idea to document items used in the spreadsheet that may not be immediately apparent, such as cell ranges and macros, so that anyone using your spreadsheet can see how your results were arrived at.

Starting Excel

Concept

To use the Microsoft Excel program, or application, the user must first open it.

Do It!

Kay wants to open the Microsoft Excel application so she can work on a worksheet.

1 Make sure the computer, monitor, and any other necessary peripheral devices are turned on. The Windows desktop should appear on your screen. Your screen may differ slightly from the one shown.

2 Locate the Windows 95 Taskbar, usually found at the bottom of your screen. Use the mouse to guide the pointer over the **Start** button, on the left side of the Taskbar, and click ▒Start . This will bring up the Windows Start menu.

3 Move the mouse pointer ⬚ up the Start menu to **Programs**, highlighting it. The Programs menu will be displayed as shown in Figure 1-3.

4 Position the pointer over **Microsoft Excel**, highlighting it, and click once to open the application. (If Excel is not there, try looking under Microsoft Office on the Start menu.) Excel will open with a blank worksheet in the window as shown in Figure 1-4.

More

Each computer can vary in its setup depending on its hardware and software configurations. Therefore, your Excel startup procedure may be slightly different from that described above. The Windows 95 environment allows you to place **shortcuts** to a program's executable (.exe) file in various places. For example, the Excel listing on the Programs menu is a shortcut. You can also place shortcuts on the desktop, or even on the first level of the Start menu. Because you can customize the Excel program, your screen may not look exactly like the one shown to the right.

Figure 1-3 Windows desktop

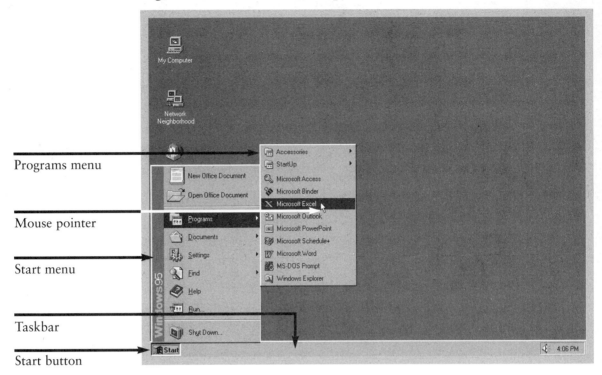

Programs menu

Mouse pointer

Start menu

Taskbar

Start button

Figure 1-4 Excel window

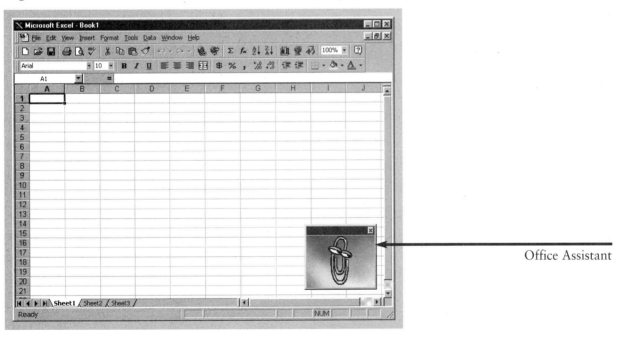

Office Assistant

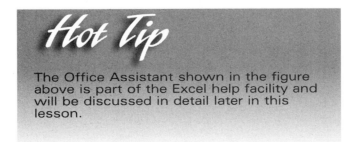

The Office Assistant shown in the figure
above is part of the Excel help facility and
will be discussed in detail later in this
lesson.

Exploring the Excel Screen

Concept

In order to begin building a spreadsheet it is necessary to become familiar with the Excel window and worksheet elements.

Do It!

To familiarize herself with the Excel screen, Kay will click on various elements of the window.

1 Click the **Maximize** button, located at the right side of the title bar, to enlarge the Excel window so that it fills your entire screen. The title bar at the top of the Excel window displays the name of the program and the title of the current worksheet that is open. When Excel opens, it automatically creates a new, empty worksheet file called Book1. The title bar also houses the Minimize, Maximize or Restore, and Close buttons used to resize the window. The Minimize button reduces the window to its program button on the Taskbar. The Maximize button will appear if the Excel window has not been enlarged to fill the entire screen, and the Restore button, which returns the window to its previous size and location, will appear if the window is maximized. Double-clicking the title bar will also maximize or restore a window.

2 Click **File** to open the File menu, then guide the pointer over each menu to familiarize yourself with the different commands. The main menu bar is usually displayed right below the title bar. The menu bar contains lists with most of Excel's commands. Each word in the menu bar can be clicked to open a pull-down menu of commands. Or, a menu may be opened by pressing the Alt key and the underlined letter in the menu name. The menu bar also contains a set of sizing buttons. These controls function in the same manner as the application sizing buttons, only they apply to the active workbook window, not the entire Excel program. You can have more than one workbook window open in the Excel program window.

3 Move the pointer over the **New** button on the Standard toolbar. A brief description of the button's function, a **ScreenTip**, will appear in a small rectangle below the button. Guide the pointer over the tool bars, pausing on each button to read its description, as shown in Figure 1-5. The two rows of icons beneath the menu bar are called toolbars. Toolbar buttons provide shortcuts to many of Excel's most commonly used commands. You can customize the toolbars to contain the tools that you use most often. The top toolbar in Figure 1-5 is called the Standard toolbar, and the lower toolbar is called the Formatting toolbar.

4 Click the **Select All** button, the gray rectangle in the upper-left corner of the worksheet where the row and column headings meet. The entire worksheet becomes highlighted, and the row and column heading buttons will become depressed. The worksheet is where you enter data to create your spreadsheet. A spreadsheet can contain may worksheets, and together multiple worksheets make up a workbook.

Figure 1-5 Elements of the Excel application window

Title bar

Menu bar

Standard toolbar

Formatting toolbar

Select All button

Cell pointer

ScreenTip

Sizing buttons

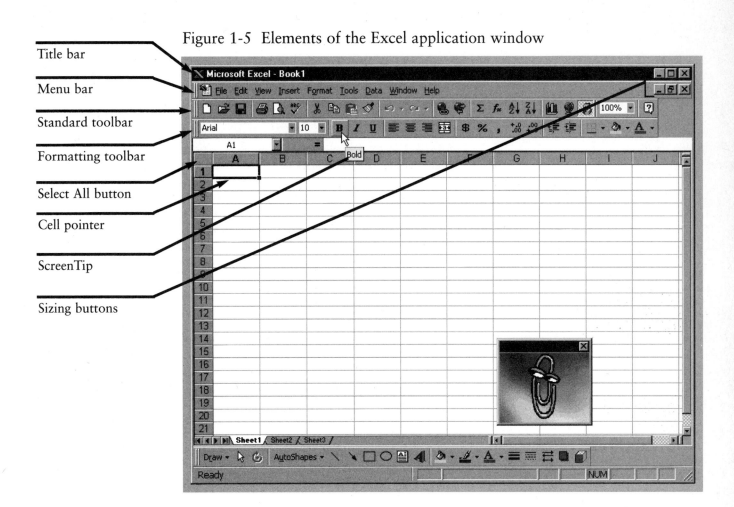

Exploring the Excel
Screen (continued)

Do It!

5 Click the letter **A** that heads the first column. Column A becomes highlighted, as shown in Figure 1-6. The columns are designated by letters, from A to Z, then AA to AZ and so on up to IV, altogether making 256 columns.

6 Click the number **1** at the left of the first row. Row 1 becomes highlighted. The rows are labeled numerically down the left side of the worksheet, from 1 to 65,536.

7 Click the intersection of column **D** and row **7**. Cell D7 is now active. Excel designates the active cell on the worksheet by bordering it with a dark rectangle called a cell pointer. Rows intersect with columns forming a grid system. Each intersection of a row and a column is called a cell. Cells are identified by an address composed of the letter and number of the column and row that intersect to form the cell. When a cell is active, you can enter new data into it or edit any data that is already there. You can make another cell active by clicking it, or by moving the cell pointer with the arrow keys found on the keyboard.

8 Click cell **H9**. Below the second row of icons are the name box and the formula bar. The name box displays the active cell address, H9, and the formula bar displays the data that you are working on, along with its location on the worksheet. The formula bar is now blank.

9 Double-click cell **H9**. At the bottom of the Excel screen is the status bar, which changes in response to the task in progress. As Figure 1-7 shows, "Enter" should now appear in the status bar indicating that you can enter a label, data, or a formula into the cell. The left side of this bar displays a brief description of Excel's current activities. The boxes to the right indicate the status of particular keys, such as the Caps Lock key.

10 Click the down arrow on the vertical scroll bar to move the spreadsheet down one row, hiding row 1. The vertical scroll bar on the far right side of the worksheet window and the horizontal scroll bar on the lower edge of the worksheet window help you move quickly around the worksheet.

11 Below the active worksheet, Excel provides sheet tabs that you can click to switch to other worksheets in the open workbook. Click the Sheet 2 tab. Notice that the cell pointer moved from H9, the active cell on Sheet 1, to cell A1, the active cell on Sheet 2. Related worksheets can be arranged together in workbooks. Book 1 in the title bar actually stands for Workbook 1. Workbooks can contain up to 255 worksheets. Sheet tab scrolling buttons (in the lower left corner of the window) help you view worksheet tabs not in the window.

Figure 1-6 Selecting a column

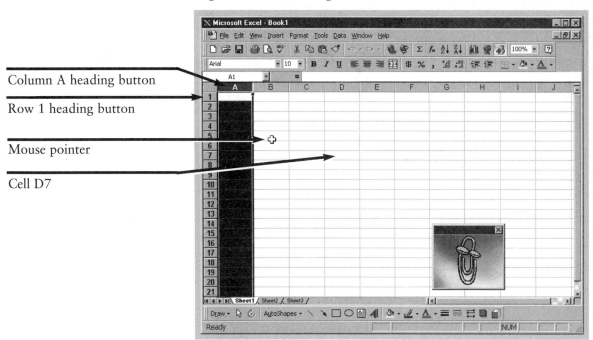

Column A heading button

Row 1 heading button

Mouse pointer

Cell D7

Figure 1-7 Components of the Excel application window

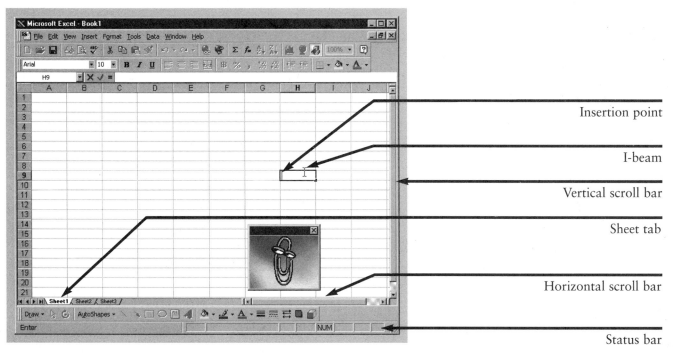

Insertion point

I-beam

Vertical scroll bar

Sheet tab

Horizontal scroll bar

Status bar

Practice

To practice what you have learned in this skill, click the Minimize button on the menu bar to minimize the document window and display it as a small title bar in the lower left of the window. Then click its Maximize button to enlarge the document.

Hot Tip

The document and application control menu icons, at the left end of the menu and title bars respectively, offer menus containing the Close and sizing commands.

Moving Around the Worksheet

Concept

To effectively use Excel you must be able to maneuver between cells in the work-space. To do this you may use either the mouse or the keyboard.

Do It!

Kay moves to various points on the Excel worksheet to familiarize herself with Excel's navigation.

1 Using the mouse, move the mouse pointer ✛ to cell **B4** and click the left mouse button. The cell becomes highlighted, marking it as the active cell.

2 Press [←]. The cell pointer moves over one cell to the left to A4.

3 Press [↑]. The cell pointer moves up one cell to A3.

4 Press the [→], then [↓] to return the cell pointer to cell B4.

5 Click once on the arrow at the right end of the horizontal scroll bar. The worksheet will scroll right by one column.

6 Scroll down one row by clicking once on the arrow at the bottom vertical scroll bar.

7 Click the horizontal scroll bar arrow until column **Z** is visible. Notice that the scroll bar box shrinks to allow you a larger movement area, as seen in Figure 1-8.

8 Click and hold the mouse button on the horizontal scroll bar box. You have now grabbed the box. Drag the box to the left until you can see column A.

Figure 1-8 Getting around the Excel application window

Name box displays selected cell, B4, even though it is not currently visible

Row 4 button bold, indicating that a cell in that row is selected

Column names extend past Z and begin again with AA, AB, etc.

Horizontal scroll bar box

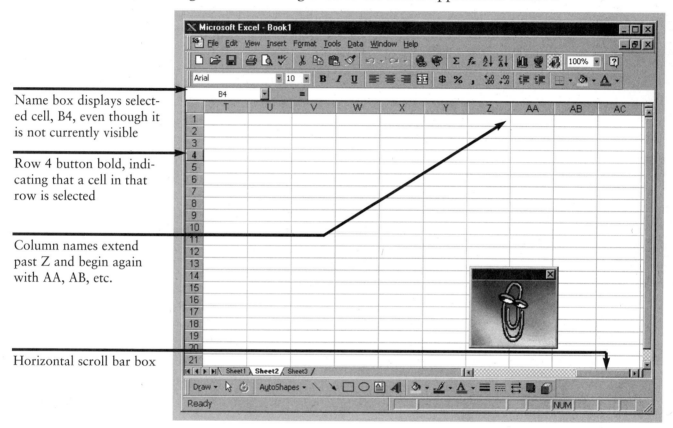

Moving Around the Worksheet (continued)

Do It!

9 Click **Edit**, then select **Go To**. The Go To dialog box, shown in Figure 1-9, appears. The Go To command is useful when you have to move a great distance across the worksheet.

10 At the bottom of the dialog box there is a text box, the white area with the flashing insertion point, labeled **Reference**. Type **Y95** in the Reference text box.

11 Click [OK]. Excel's cell pointer highlights cell Y95 in the worksheet.

12 Press [**Ctrl**]+[**Home**]. The cell pointer will jump to cell A1. The [Ctrl]+[Home] command is helpful for returning to the beginning of a worksheet.

More

At the bottom of the worksheet are three **tabs** labeled Sheet1, Sheet2, and Sheet3. A workbook is often made up of many **worksheets**, and each tab corresponds to a different worksheet. Interrelated data can be kept across multiple worksheets of the same workbook for viewing, cross referencing, and calculation. To go to a different worksheet, simply click its tab at the bottom of the window. New worksheets can be added to a workbook by using the Worksheet command on the Insert menu. The new worksheet will appear before the active worksheet. You can move a worksheet to a different place in the worksheet hierarchy by dragging its tab to the desired place in the row of tabs. The mouse pointer will appear with a blank sheet attached to it ⬡ and a small arrow ▼ will indicate where the worksheet will be placed when you release the mouse button. The tab scrolling buttons ◖◀ ▶ ▶◗, located to the left of the sheet tabs, allow you to view tabs that do not fit in the window. Clicking one of the outer buttons moves to the beginning or end of the list of tabs, while clicking one of the inner buttons will move one at a time through the tabs. If you right-click the tab scrolling buttons, a pop-up menu listing all of the tabs in your workbook will appear, allowing you to select a specific tab to jump to. Tabs can be renamed by double-clicking the tab to select its text, and then editing it like normal text.

Table 1-1   Moving in a Worksheet

MOVEMENT	ACTION
Left one cell	Press [←] or [Shift]+[Tab]
Right one cell	Press [→] or [Tab]
Up one cell	Press [↑] or [Shift]+[Enter]
Down one cell	Press [↓] or [Enter]
Left one column or right one column	Click the left arrow or right arrow on the horizontal scroll bar
Up one row or down one row	Click the up arrow or down arrow on the vertical scroll bar
Up one screen or down one screen	Press [Page Up] or [Page Down]
Left one screen or right one screen	Press [Alt]+[Page Up] or [Alt]+[Page Down]
Go to cell A1	[Ctrl]+[Home]
Go to column A in current row	[Home]

Figure 1-9 Go To dialog box

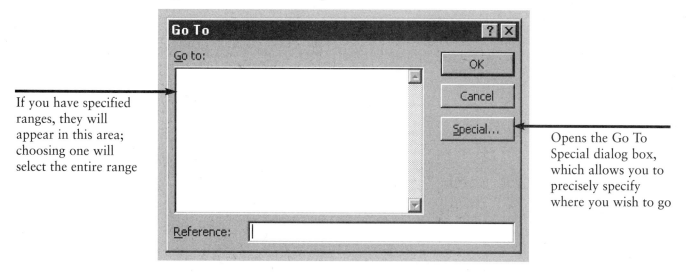

If you have specified ranges, they will appear in this area; choosing one will select the entire range

Opens the Go To Special dialog box, which allows you to precisely specify where you wish to go

Practice

Click cell E12 to make it active, then use the arrow keys to move the cell pointer to cell G7. Open the Go To dialog box and navigate to cell CT2041. Finally, position the cell pointer in cell A1.

Hot Tip

To move across a large area of blank cells press [End]; the word END will appear in the status bar. Then press an arrow key. The cell pointer will jump to the next filled cell in the direction of the arrow key pressed.

Entering Labels

Concept

Labels are used to annotate and describe the data you place into rows and columns. Properly labeled data makes your spreadsheet easy to understand and interpret. Labels can consist of text or numbers and are aligned left so as to differentiate them from data used in calculations. Excel automatically left-justifies labels. Labels should be entered into your spreadsheet first so that your rows and columns are defined before your begin to enter the calculable data.

Do It!

Kay enters the documentation and row labels for her spreadsheet.

1 Click cell **A2** to make it the active cell. The address A2 appears in the name box.

2 Type **Income and Expenditures for Kay's Hound Accessories**, then click the **Enter** button ☑. The label will appear in the formula bar as you type. Even though the label is longer than the cell width, it will be displayed in its entirety as long as the next cell remains empty.

3 Click cell **A3** and type **File name: Profit1.xls**, then press [**Enter**]. The label will be entered and the cell pointer will move down one row to cell A4.

4 Type **Author: Kay Samoy**, click cell **D4** and type **Date: 4/6/98**. In cell **A5** type **Ranges:**, in cell **D5** type **Macros:**, and in cell **F5** type **Assumptions: Sales Growth**. These labels are the documentation for your spreadsheet. Documentation describes and titles your spreadsheet. It contains the purpose, file name, and author of the spreadsheets, and the date it was created, as well as defining any ranges, macros, and assumptions that it may contain.

5 Click cell **A8** to make it the active cell. Type **Income** and then press [**Enter**]. The next six labels will be the row headings.

6 Type **Sales**, then press [**Enter**]; skip a cell and in cell **A11** type **Expenditures**, then press [**Enter**]; in cell **A12** type **Rent**, then press [**Enter**]; in cell **A13** type **Salaries**, then press [**Enter**]; in cell **A14** type **Misc.**, then press [**Enter**]; and in cell **A15** type **Total Expenses**, then press [**Enter**]. Your worksheet should now look like the one shown in Figure 1-10.

More

Then Enter button on the formula bar functions in much the same way as the Enter key on the keyboard, but after you click the Enter button, the cell pointer remains in the current cell instead of moving to the cell beneath. The Enter button disappears after you use it, but you can bring it back by clicking the text box on the formula bar. The **Cancel** button ☒ not only removes the contents from a cell, but also restores the cell's previous contents, if there were any.

Excel automatically assumes that a number is a value and aligns it to the right by default. If you wish to use a number as a label, simply type an apostrophe ['] before the number. The data will then be aligned to the left. The apostrophe will be hidden in the cell, but will be shown in the formula bar.

Figure 1-10 Entering labels

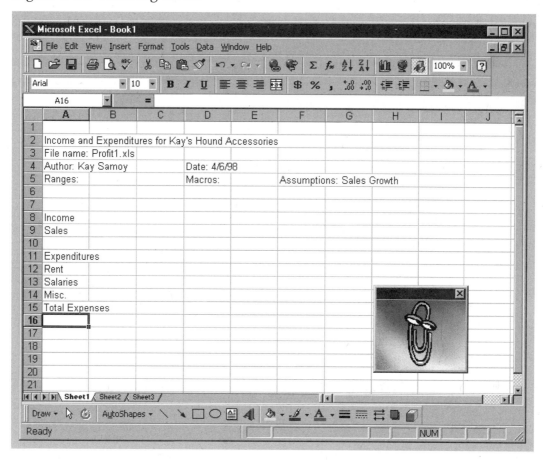

Practice

Click the **New** button 🗋 to open a new workbook. Beginning in cell A2, enter the following information as cell labels, pressing **[Enter]** after each: your name, today's date, your instructor's name, and the title of this course.

Hot Tip

If you start to enter a label whose first few letters match those of an adjacent cell in the column, Excel will automatically complete the label to match. If you do not wish to accept the suggestion, simply continue typing to overwrite Excel's suggestion.

Skill *Skill* Saving and Closing a Worksheet

Concept

Saving your work is important; if not saved, work can be lost due to power or computer failure. Once a file has been saved, it can be reopened at any time for editing or viewing. Your workbook can be saved to a hard drive, floppy disk, or network drive. **Closing** a file removes it from the screen and puts it away for later use. You can close a file while leaving the application open for use with other Excel files. Or, if you are finished using Excel, you can exit the application.

Do It!

Kay wants to save her worksheet under the name Profit1 in a folder titled Kay's Hound Accessories.

1 Click **Window**, then select **Book1.xls** from the menu if it is not already active. Book1.xls will become the active document.

2 Click **File**, then click **Save As**. Notice that the Save As command is followed by an ellipsis (three dots), indicating that a dialog box will open when the command is executed. The Save As dialog box opens, as shown in Figure 1-11. (If you had chosen the Save command, the Save As dialog would have appeared anyway, since this is the first time you will be saving your document.) The file name Book1.xls automatically appears highlighted in the File Name text box, ready to be changed.

3 To give the workbook file a more distinctive name, type **Profit1**. The .xls file extension will automatically be added. As you type the name, Book1.xls will be overwritten. Windows 95 supports file names of up to 255 characters. The file name can contain upper or lower case letters, numbers, and most symbols.

4 Click the **Save in** list arrow to choose where to save the file. Excel is programmed to save newly created files in the My Documents folder by default. Click **3½ Floppy (A:)** if your student files will be stored on a floppy disk or **Maindisk (C:)** if your student files are to be stored on your hard drive. Consult with your instructor about which drive to use.

5 Click the **Create New Folder** button ⬜. The New Folder dialog box will appear with the folder name New Folder highlighted in the Name text box, as shown in Figure 1-12.

Figure 1-11 Save As dialog box

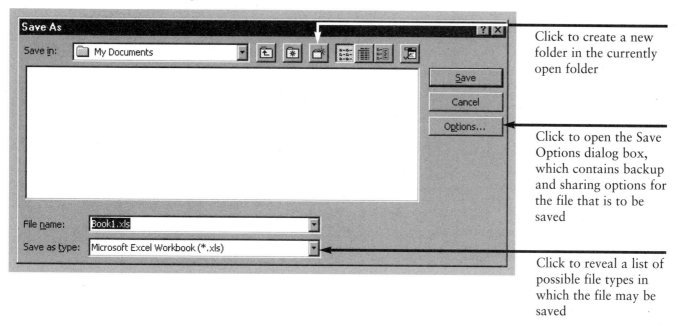

Click to create a new folder in the currently open folder

Click to open the Save Options dialog box, which contains backup and sharing options for the file that is to be saved

Click to reveal a list of possible file types in which the file may be saved

Figure 1-12 New Folder dialog box

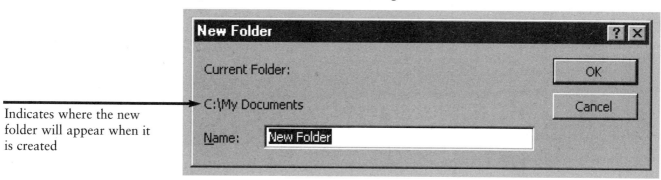

Indicates where the new folder will appear when it is created

Saving and Closing a Worksheet (continued)

Do It!

6 Type **Kay's Hound Accessories**. The default name will be replaced with the new text.

7 Click [OK]. The new folder will be created in the Save As dialog box.

8 Click Kay's folder to select it. It will become highlighted.

9 Click the **Open** button [Open]. The selection area will appear blank since there are no files or folders in Kay's folder, as shown in Figure 1-13.

10 Click [Save] to store the worksheet in Kay's folder. The Save As dialog box will close and the new file name will appear on the title bar.

11 Click **File**, then click **Close**. The workbook file is removed from the Excel window.

More

You can also use the **AutoSave** option to have Excel automatically save your file every few minutes. The AutoSave command is found on the Tools menu. If it is not there, you will have to install the AutoSave add-in. Select the Add-In command from the Tools menu to open the Add-Ins dialog box. Click the check box next to AutoSave, and then click the OK button. After Excel has set up the AutoSave feature, select it from the Tools menu; the AutoSave dialog box will open. You can turn AutoSave on or off with the check box at the top left of the dialog box, and can choose the time between saves by entering an interval in the text box labeled minutes. You have the option of saving just the active workbook or all of the open workbooks, and Excel can prompt you before it auto saves if you wish, so as to avoid inadvertently saving unwanted changes.

Table 1-2   Save As dialog box buttons

BUTTON	NAME	FUNCTION
	Up One Level	Takes you up one level in the file hierarchy
	Look in Favorites	Takes you to the Favorites folder where you can store documents you use frequently
	Create New Folder	Allows you to make a new folder
	List	Allows you to view files or folders in a simple list form
	Details	Allows you to view files or folders and their specific attributes such as size and type
	Properties	Allows you to view file or folder properties
	Commands and Settings	Offers a menu of advanced functions such as sorting and mapping a network drive

Figure 1-13 Saving a file in a new folder

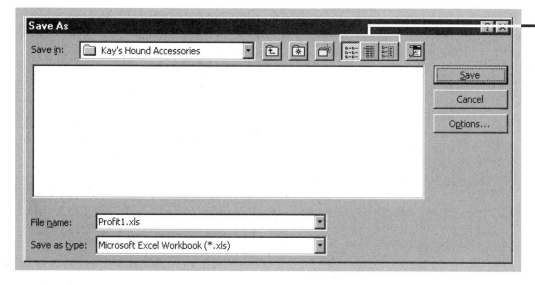

View buttons that control the way files are displayed in the list

Practice

Save the workbook you created in the practice for the previous skill onto your student disk as Practice1-7 and then close the workbook.

Hot Tip

If you do not save your workbook file, the data will be lost when you exit the program or turn your computer off. To quickly save a file that has already been named, use the Save button on the Standard toolbar or use the keyboard and press [Ctrl]+[S].

 Opening a Worksheet

Concept

In order to work with a saved file you must first **open** it. Opening a file requires that you know the file's name and the location where it is stored.

Do It!

Kay needs to open her file so that she can edit one of the labels.

1 Click **File**, then click **Open**. Notice that the Open command is followed by an ellipsis (three dots) indicating that a dialog box will open, since the command requires more information. The Open dialog box will appear as shown in Figure 1-14.

2 Earlier you saved the file Profit1 in a folder named Kay's Hound Accessories. Click the **Look in** drop down list arrow and select the drive where your student files are stored. Insert your Student Disk into the A: drive and click the 3½ Floppy (A:) if they are stored on a floppy, or click Maindisk (C:) if they are in a folder on your hard disk. A list of the files and folders on the drive will appear in the list box.

3 Click the folder named **Kay's Hound Accessories**, then click the **Open** button ⬚. The files housed in the folder will appear in the contents window.

4 Double-click the **Profit1** file. The Open dialog box disappears and the worksheet will be displayed in the Excel window as shown in Figure 1-15.

More

Word's search abilities are immense. The **Text or property** text box allows you to search for documents containing specific words or characters by entering the text fragment in the Text or property text box within quotation marks. Without quotation marks, Word will search for documents whose Properties dialog box contains the entered text. The **Last modified** text box lets you restrict the search to documents modified yesterday, last week, and so on.

If you are connected to an Internet provider, you can search the Web by clicking the **Search the Web** button ⬚. Clicking this button calls up your Web browser and takes you to a search page. By searching the Web by topic or keyword, a search engine will provide you with an organized list of links to relevant Web sights. There is also a **Web toolbar** that contains the Search the Web button, as well as providing a text box in which you can specify a URL that you would like to go to.

Figure 1-14 Open dialog box

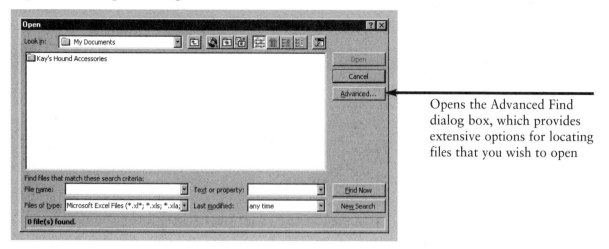

Opens the Advanced Find dialog box, which provides extensive options for locating files that you wish to open

Figure 1-15 Opening a previously saved file

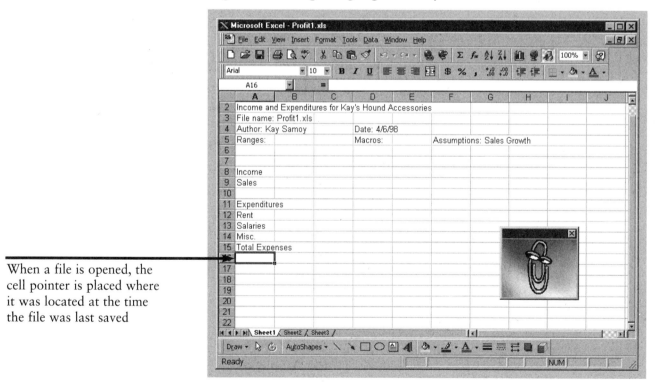

When a file is opened, the cell pointer is placed where it was located at the time the file was last saved

Practice

To practice opening Excel documents, open the student file **Practice-Lesson 1.xls**. Then save it to your student disk as **MyPractice 1**.

Hot Tip

When searching for files from the Open dialog box, you can click the Commands and Settings button, then click Search Subfolders to expand your search to all folders in the hierarchy rather than only the selected level.

 # Editing a Cell's Information

Concept

Information entered into a cell is not permanent. You can change, or edit, the contents of a cell at any time.

Do It!

Kay wants to edit cell A11 to change Expenditures to Expenses.

1 Click cell **A11**. The cell pointer moves to cell A11 and Expenditures is displayed in the formula bar.

2 Move the mouse pointer from the worksheet to the formula bar and position it between the n and the d of the word **Expenditures** (the pointer will change from a cross ✚ to an I-beam ⌶) and click. A blinking insertion point will appear, the formula bar buttons will be displayed, and the mode indicator on the status bar will read Edit, as shown in Figure 1-16.

3 Click and hold the left mouse button, then drag the I-beam to the right, over the last seven letters of the word **Expenditures**. The rest of the formula bar will become highlighted. Highlighting, or selecting, text allows it to be edited.

4 Type **ses** and then click the **Enter** button ☑ . The new text will replace the incorrect label and the spreadsheet will look like Figure 1-17.

5 Save your workbook by clicking the **Save** button 🖫 .

More

Excel provides you with multiple ways to edit a cell's information. You can select the cell you wish to edit and then click the formula bar, as described above. You can also double-click a desired cell, making a flashing insertion point appear. Then you can use the backspace and/or delete keys to remove the character to the left or right of the insertion point respectively, and the keyboard to edit the cell. Or, you can double-click a second time to highlight all of the cell's contents and edit the selection. Finally, you can select a cell and then press [F2], again making the insertion point appear in the selected cell.

Figure 1-16 Editing a cell label

Place the insertion point with the mouse

Contents of the selected cell appear above in the Formula bar

Indicates that Excel is in edit mode, allowing you to change the contents of the selected cell

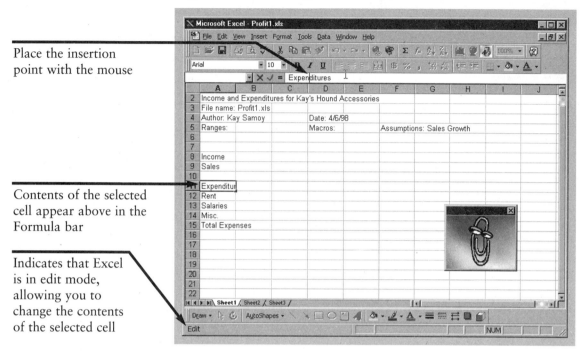

Figure 1-17 Changed cell label

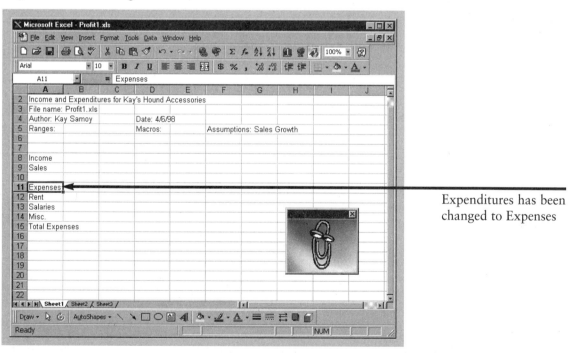

Expenditures has been changed to Expenses

Practice

To practice editing cell information, go to the Prac1-9 tab of the **MyPractice 1** student file.

Hot Tip

The Undo button on the Standard toolbar will cancel the last action taken. Clicking the Undo drop-down list arrow opens a list of recent commands and actions; clicking one will undo all actions back to and including the selected one.

Using the Office Assistant

Concept

Even the most experienced users need help from time to time. The **Office Assistant** is a help facility that lets you ask a question relating to your problem, and will reply with several help options that may be useful to you based on the question you asked.

Do It!

Kay has questions about Excel. She will use the **Office Assistant** to find out about some of Excel's capabilities.

1 Click the Office Assistant's window. Its dialog balloon appears with the text "Type your question here, and then click Search" selected.

2 In the text box, type **What does the Office Assistant do?** and then click ⊙ Search. A list of topics appears in the balloon, as shown in Figure 1-18.

3 Click the first topic, **Get Help, tips, and messages through the Office Assistant.** Figure 1-19 shows the Microsoft Excel dialog box that appears.

4 Read the Help topic pertaining to the Office Assistant, clicking a few of the help buttons ≫ next to additional topics to find out more.

5 When you have finished reading about some of the Office Assistant's capabilities, click the **Close** button in the upper right corner of the dialog box.

6 Click the **Close** button in the Office Assistant's window to hide the Assistant.

More

From time to time the Assistant will offer you tips on how to use Excel more efficiently. The appearance of a small light bulb, either in the Assistant's window or on the Office Assistant button, indicates that there is a tip to be viewed. To see the tip, click the light bulb in whichever location it appears.

The Office Assistant can be customized. Click the ⊙ Options button in its dialog balloon to open the Office Assistant dialog box. This dialog box has two tabs: Gallery and Options. The **Gallery** tab contains nine assistants you can choose from, and scrolling through the characters provides you with a preview of each one. From the **Options** tab, shown in Figure 1-20, you can alter the Assistant's capabilities and decide what kinds of tips it will show.

Figure 1-18 Assistant's search results

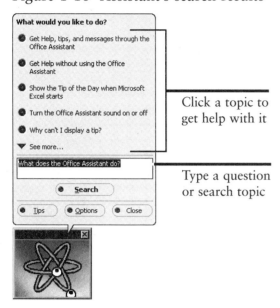

Click a topic to get help with it

Type a question or search topic

Figure 1-19 Help with the Office Assistant

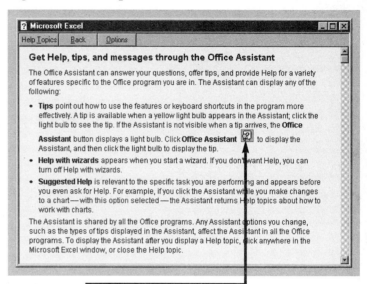

Click this icon to bring up
a definition of the word
with which it is associated

Figure 1-20 Office Assistant dialog box

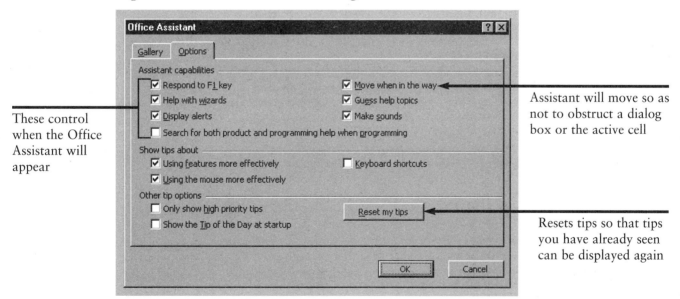

These control
when the Office
Assistant will
appear

Assistant will move so as
not to obstruct a dialog
box or the active cell

Resets tips so that tips
you have already seen
can be displayed again

Practice

Use the Office Assistant to learn about moving the Office Assistant and its balloon.

Hot Tip

The Office Assistant is common to all Office 97 applications. Therefore, any Assistant options you change will affect it in all Office programs.

Getting Help in Excel

Concept

Excel has more traditional help facilities that are easily searched if you know what you are looking for. The Help menu contains a **Contents** feature that organizes information by category, and an **Index** that lists all help topics alphabetically.

Do It!

Kay wants to use the Index to find out more about ScreenTips.

1. Click **Help,** then click **Contents and Index.** The Help Topics: Microsoft Excel dialog box opens.

2. Click the **Index** tab to bring it to the front, as shown in Figure 1-21.

3. Type **ScreenT.** The Index scrolls as you type, anticipating your selection. ScreenTips appears highlighted on the list.

4. Click Display . A Microsoft Excel dialog box appears with a selection of help topics arranged across a picture of the Office Assistant. (See Figure 1-22.)

5. Click ScreenTips . A large ScreenTip appears explaining various ways to access ScreenTips while you work.

6. When you are finished reading about ScreenTips, click the window's **Close** button.

More

The Index tab of the Help Topics dialog box is very helpful if you know what the task you are trying to accomplish is called, or if you know the name of the feature that you want to find out more about. If you are unsure of exactly what you are looking for, the **Contents** tab of the Help Topics dialog box may be a better option for you. The Contents feature contains every Help topic that Excel offers, broken down by category, and is useful if you want to obtain a broad view of the topics available. The **Find** tab allows you to search for key words found in Help topics to pinpoint those topics that might be most helpful.

Figure 1-21 Index tab of the Help Topics dialog box

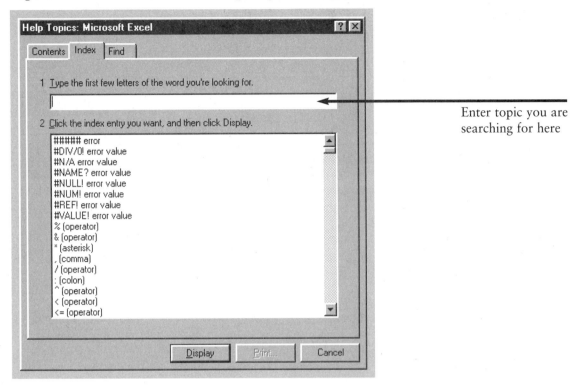

Enter topic you are
searching for here

Figure 1-22 Microsoft Excel help topic

Click to open the Index

Clicking a flagged item such as
this opens a large ScreenTip to
more thoroughly explain the
topic

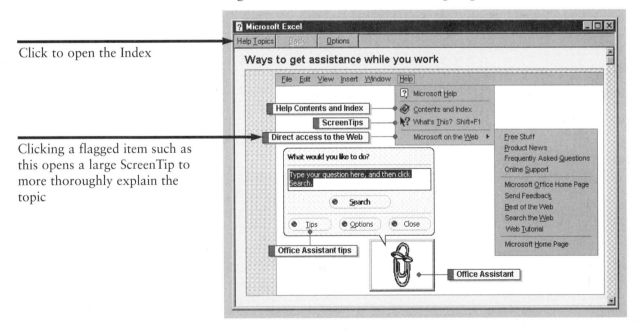

Practice

Use the Index to find shortcut keys that
relate to the Office Assistant.

Hot Tip

If your computer is connected to the
Internet, you can access Microsoft's Web
pages directly from Excel. Highlight
Microsoft on the Web on the Help menu,
and then click a topic to go to its Web
page.

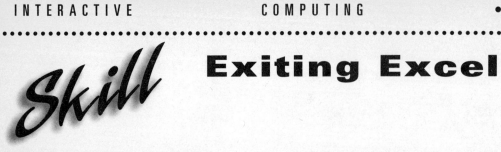

Exiting Excel

Concept

It is important to properly exit the Excel program when you are finished with the day's session. Correctly closing the application will help you avoid any data loss.

Do It!

Kay has finished using Excel for the day and is ready to exit the application.

1 Click **File,** then click **Close.** Since you have altered the spreadsheet since the last time you saved, a dialog box will open asking if you want to "Save changes in 'Profit1.xls'?"

2 Click [Yes]. Excel will save the changes you have made and the worksheet will disappear from the window.

3 To close the application click **File,** then click **Exit.** (See Figure 1-23.) Excel closes and removes itself from the desktop.

More

There are other ways you can close a file and exit Excel. The easiest method is to use the **Close** buttons ☒ located in the upper right corner of the window. The Close button on the menu bar is for the active workbook, and the Close button on the title bar is for the application.

You can open any menu on the menu bar by pressing the [Alt] key followed by the underlined letter in the menu's title. You will notice that menu commands also have a letter in their name underlined; typing the underlined letter will activate its command on the open menu. For example, with the File menu open, typing a [c] will close the file and pressing [x] will exit Excel.

Figure 1-23 Closing the Excel Application

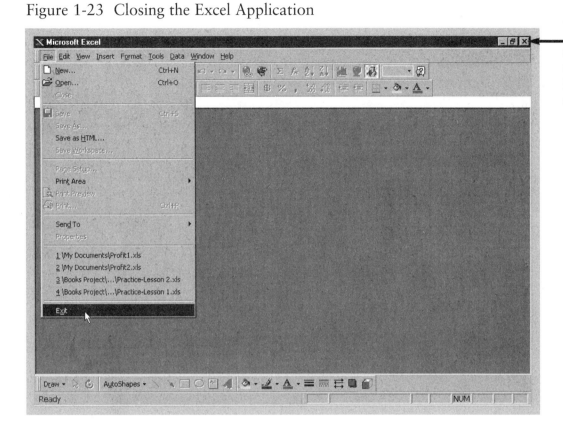

Clicking this Close button will likewise exit the application

Practice

Open Excel, then exit the application by clicking the Close button ⊠ on the title bar.

Hot Tip

Pressing the [Ctrl] key plus [W] will close your file, while [Alt] + [F4] is the key combination used to exit Excel.

Shortcuts

Function	Button/Mouse	Menu	Keyboard
Create a new file		Click File, then click New	[Ctrl]+[N]
Open a file		Click File, then click Open	[Ctrl]+[O]
Maximize a window		Click Control icon, then click Maximize	
Minimize a window		Click Control icon, then click Minimize	
Restore a window		Click Control icon, then click Restore	
Close a window		Click Control icon, then click Close	[Alt]+[F4] (application) [Ctrl]+[W] (document)
Confirm a cell entry			[Enter], [Tab], arrow keys
Cancel a cell entry		Click Edit, then click Undo typing	[Ctrl]+[Z]
Search the Web (from the Open dialog box)			
Save a file		Click File, then click Save	[Ctrl]+[S]
Office Assistant		Click Help, then click Microsoft Excel Help	[F1]
What's This?		Click Help, then click What's This?	[Shift]+[F1]

Identify Key Features

Figure 1-24 Identify elements of the Excel screen

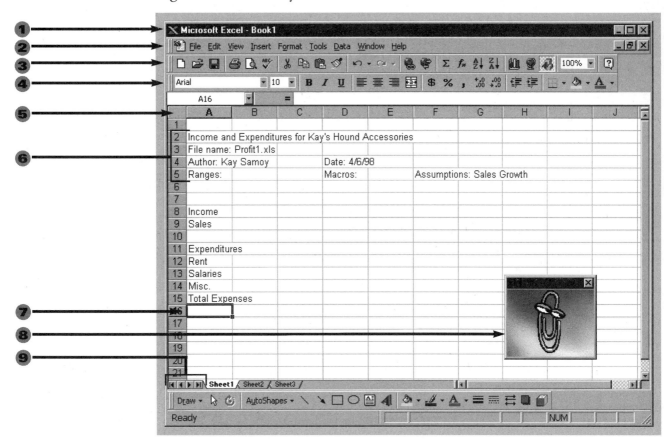

Select the Best Answer

10. Click this to make the Excel window fill the screen

11. Displays the active cell address

12. Displays a brief description of your current activities in Excel

13. Allows you to choose a name and location for storing a file

14. Saves your file keeping its current name and location

a. Name box

b. Save button

c. Maximize button

d. Status bar

e. Save As command

Quiz (continued)

Complete the Statement

15. To select an entire column, click:

    a. The first cell in the column

    b. Any cell in the column

    c. Its letter column heading

    d. The corresponding row number

16. Text or numbers that describe your data are called:

    a. Annotations

    b. Ranges

    c. Justifications

    d. Labels

17. Pressing [Ctrl]+[Home] will:

    a. Move your view up one screen

    b. Move your view down one screen

    c. Move the cell pointer to cell A1

    d. Move the cell pointer to Column A in the current row

18. A well-designed spreadsheet does not require:

    a. Documentation

    b. Multiple worksheets

    c. Input

    d. Output

19. All of these are Excel Help facilities except:

    a. The Index

    b. The Office Assistant

    c. What's This?

    d. The HelpWizard

20. All of the following actions will move the cell pointer to another cell except:

    a. Clicking the Enter button

    b. Pressing the Enter key

    c. Pressing the Tab key

    d. Pressing an arrow key

Interactivity

Test Your Skills

1. Open the Excel application and document a new spreadsheet:

   a. Use the Start button to launch Microsoft Excel.

   b. Add a documentation section to the blank worksheet using the title **Class Schedule,** your name, and the date.

   c. When you document the file name, use the name **Test 1.xls.**

   d. Include labels for ranges and macros. Your documentation section should occupy Rows 1-4 of the worksheet.

2. Design a worksheet that displays your daily class schedule:

   a. Add labels in row 6 for the days of the week. Start in cell B6, and skip a column between each day. **Friday** should be in cell J6.

   b. Add labels in column A for your class periods. Enter the time of your earliest class in cell A8, and then add a label for each subsequent class period through your last class of the day. Skip a row between each time label.

   c. Enter the names of your classes in the appropriate cells where the day of the week and the time intersect.

3. Get help from the Office Assistant:

   a. Open the Office Assistant's dialog balloon.

   b. Ask the Assistant for information on how to **customize toolbars.**

   c. Choose a topic that the Assistant provides, and then read the information in the Help window.

   d. Close the Help window when you are done, and then close the Office Assistant's window.

4. Save your file and exit Excel:

   a. Save your spreadsheet under the name **Test 1.xls.**

   b. Exit Microsoft Excel.

Problem Solving

Create a new spreadsheet following the design principles you learned in Lesson 1. Design this spreadsheet to log your daily activities. Enter labels for the days of the week just as you did in the previous exercise, but this time add Saturday and Sunday after Friday, and do not leave a blank column between each day. Instead of class periods, add labels down column A for **Class, Activities, Meals, Studying/Homework, Leisure,** and **Sleep.** Do not skip rows between labels. Save the file as **Solved 1.xls.**

Skills

L E S S O N

2

MANIPULATING DATA IN A WORKSHEET

One of the greatest advantages of using spreadsheet software is that it automates many of the processes that take up so much time when done by hand. In Excel, you can move or copy data from one location in a worksheet to another quickly and easily.

Excel also automates your calculations by using mathematical formulas. If you instruct Excel what operation to perform, and where to get the data, the program will execute the calculations for you. The Paste Function feature prevents you from having to enter complicated formulas that Excel already knows. Once you have entered a formula or a function, you can even paste it into a new location.

Companies often like to use the data they have gathered to make projections about their business. In Excel, you can use assumptions to perform calculations under different conditions, altering the results of the worksheet each time. This technique is known as what-if analysis, and takes full advantage of Excel's versatility.

Case Study:
In this lesson, Kay will use Excel's Cut, Copy, and Paste features to manipulate the labels in her spreadsheet. She will also fill out the worksheet with values, and then use those values to perform calculations using formulas and functions. Then she will change her output by performing a what-if analysis. Finally, Kay will print a copy of her worksheet.

Cutting, Copying, and Pasting Data

Concept

Excel makes it easy to transfer data from cell to cell. **Cutting** or **copying** information places it on the Windows **Clipboard**, a temporary storage place for data. The **Paste** command inserts the contents of the Clipboard at the insertion point. Cell contents may also be moved by dragging and dropping with the mouse.

Do It!

Kay wants to add the column heading Quarter in four cells, B6, C6, D6, and E6 of her spreadsheet. Then she will cut and paste the column headings from row 6 to row 7.

1 Open Excel by clicking the **Start** button, then selecting **Excel** from the Programs menu. The Excel window will appear on your desktop.

2 Click the **Open** button 📂, then find the folder named Kay's Hound Accessories, and open **Profit1.xls**. Your workbook will appear in the Excel window.

3 Click cell **B6**. The cell pointer will appear in cell B6 to indicated it is active.

4 Type **Quarter**, then click the **Enter** button ✅ to confirm the entry. The label will appear in cell B6.

5 Click **Edit**, then click **Copy** to send a duplicate of the contents of the selected cell to the Clipboard. An animated dashed border appears around the copied selection, as shown in Figure 2-1.

6 Press [**Tab**] to move the cell pointer to cell **C6**. Notice that the animated border remains in cell B6.

7 Click **Edit** then click **Paste** to insert the copied text into the selected cell.

8 Move the mouse pointer to the fill handle, the black square in the lower right corner of the cell, until it changes to a crosshair ➕ indicating that the selection can be copied elsewhere in the document.

9 Click the left mouse button and drag the fill pointer to cell **E6**. The cells will appear with a gray border, identifying them as a possible destination for the copied data, and a ScreenTip displaying the text to be copied will appear, as seen in Figure 2-2.

10 Release the mouse button. A copy of the selected data will appear in cells D6 and E6.

Figure 2-1 Copying a cell

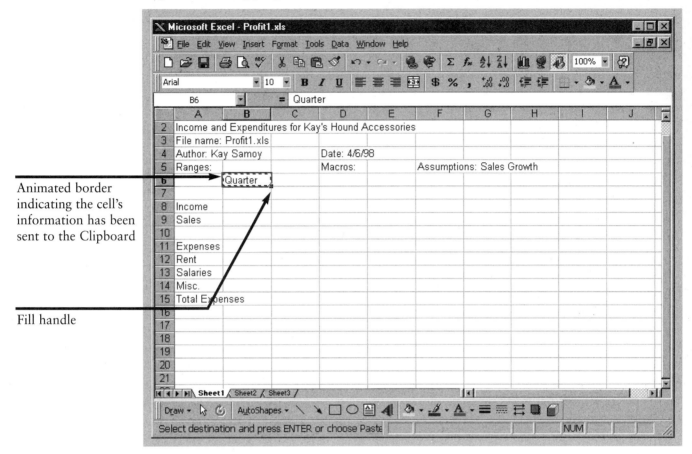

Animated border indicating the cell's information has been sent to the Clipboard

Fill handle

Figure 2-2 Selected destination cells

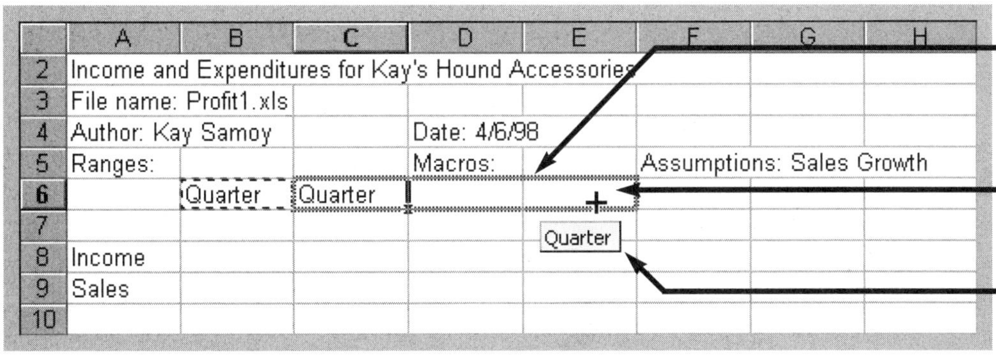

Cells to be filled are indicated by a gray border

Fill pointer

A ScreenTip displays what will be copied

Cutting, Copying, and Pasting Data (continued)

Do It!

11 Double-click cell **B6** to put it into edit mode. Edit will appear in the status bar.

12 Place the I-beam after Quarter, press [**Space**], then type [**1**]. The label will read Quarter 1.

13 Repeat the previous steps so that cells C6 through E6 read Quarter 2 thorough 4 respectively. Your worksheet should now resemble the one in Figure 2-3.

14 Click cell **B6** to select it, then drag the mouse pointer to cell **E6** so that all four cells are encompassed in the cell pointer. Cells C6, D6, and E6 will be highlighted.

15 Click the **Cut** button 🔲 on the Standard toolbar. The column headings are surrounded by an animated border.

16 Click cell **B7**, then drag to cell **E7** to select the entire group as the destination cells for the cut information.

17 Click the **Paste** button 🔲. The column headings in row 6 will be pasted into row 7, as shown in Figure 2-4.

18 Save your worksheet by clicking the **Save** button 🔲.

More

You can move or copy a cell's contents with the mouse by **dragging and dropping**. Dragging involves positioning the pointer over an object, clicking the left mouse button to grab the object, and then moving the mouse, and the object, to a new location. When the mouse pointer is over a cell pointer it will change to an arrow. You can then click and drag the cell pointer to a new location to move the contents of the selected cell or cells without having to use the Clipboard. Releasing the mouse button drops a grabbed object into place. Pressing [Ctrl] while dragging and dropping causes the pointer to change to the copy pointer 🔲. When dropped, the contents of the selection will appear in the new location but the original information will remain intact.

If you want to fill a range of cells with copies of a selected cell or cells, move the mouse pointer to the **fill handle**, the square at the bottom right corner of a cell pointer, until it changes to a crosshair. Then click and drag the mouse pointer in the direction of the columns or rows that you wish to fill; a gray border will appear around the cells that will be filled with copies of your original selection when you release the mouse button. Using the fill handle allows you to make multiple copies of a selected cell's or cells' contents at the same time, whereas you can only make a single copy of a cell's contents using the drag-and-drop method described above.

The Clipboard is only a temporary storage device for cut or copied information, and once a new item is cut or copied it will replace the previous item. You can use the Clipboard to transfer text, graphics, and other objects between worksheets, files, and even applications.

Figure 2-3 Edited cells

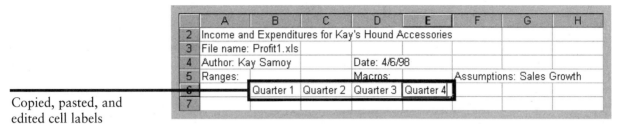

Copied, pasted, and
edited cell labels

Figure 2-4 Cut and pasted cells

Cut button

Paste button

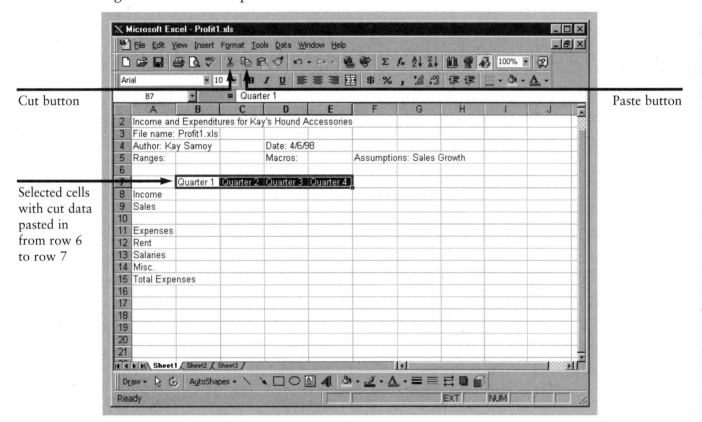

Selected cells
with cut data
pasted in
from row 6
to row 7

Practice

Open the practice file **Practice-Lesson 2.xls**, save it as **MyPractice2**, and then follow the instructions on the **Prac2-1** sheet.

Hot Tip

The Clipboard is cleared when Windows 95 is shut down or the computer is turned off.

# Entering Values

Concept

Values are numbers, formulas, or functions that Excel uses in calculations. They must be entered and confirmed in the same way that labels are.

Do It!

Kay wants to enter sales and expense values into her worksheet.

1 Click cell **B9** to make it the active cell.

2 Type **970000**, then press [**Tab**]. The first quarter sales value is entered into the cell and the cell pointer moves to the right to cell C9.

3 Now enter the rest of the Sales values in the row, pressing [**Tab**] after each: **1000400, 1210305, 1484032.**

4 Click cell **B12** to activate it.

5 Type **45000** and then click the **Enter** button ☑.

6 Since the rent is the same for each quarter, copy the data in cell **B12** and paste it into the other three cells in the row; **C12, D12,** and **E12,** by clicking on the fill handle, dragging it to cell **E12,** and then releasing it. Notice the ScreenTip that shows the data that will be copied.

7 Click cell **B13** to activate it and enter the following four values into the **Salaries** row, pressing [**Tab**] after each: **30000, 30000, 51750, 61750.**

8 Click cell **B14** to activate it and enter the following four Misc. values into the row, pressing [**Tab**] after each: **10200, 8188, 7900, 9940.** Your worksheet should now resemble the one shown in Figure 2-5.

More

You may have noticed that the values you entered, unlike labels, were aligned to the right when confirmed. Excel aligns values to the right by default, and recognizes an entry as a value when it is a number or is preceded by +, -, =, @, #, or $. Ordinals (1st, 2nd, 3rd, etc.) and other combinations of numbers and letters are recognized as labels. Sometimes you may want to use a number, such as a year, as a label; in this case, you can type an apostrophe (') before it to make Excel recognize it as a label and disregard it when performing calculations. The apostrophe will not be visible in the cell, but will be shown in the formula bar when the cell is selected.

Figure 2-5 Entering values into the worksheet

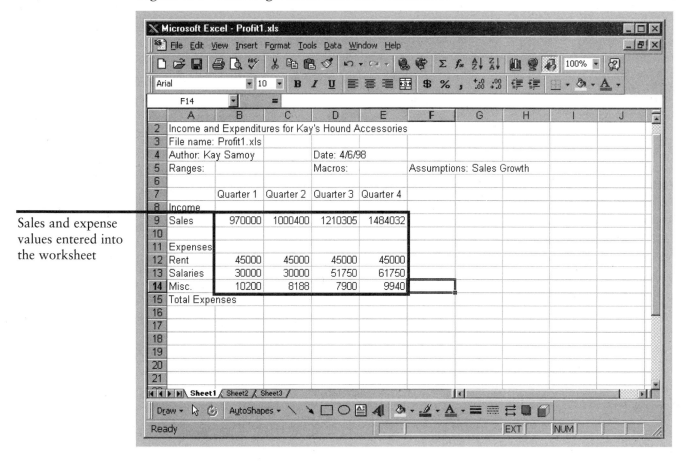

Sales and expense values entered into the worksheet

Practice

To practice entering values, follow the instructions on the **Prac2-2** tab of the practice file **MyPractice 2.xls**.

Hot Tip

If you want to use the numeric keypad to enter numbers into a cell, the Num Lock must be on.

 **Entering Formulas**

Concept

Formulas allow Excel to perform calculations such as averages, sums, or products using values that have been entered into the worksheet.

Do It!

Kay would like to calculate the total expenses and profits for each quarter.

1. Click cell **B15** to activate it. This is the cell where the formula will be entered, and where the calculated result will appear.

2. Enter the following formula into the active cell: **=B12+B13+B14**. Notice that part of the label Total Expenses in cell A15 disappeared. You will learn how to widen columns in Lesson 3. The equals sign preceding the cell addresses and arithmetical operators prompts Excel to recognize the information as a formula. This calculation will result in a sum of the values in the three cells referenced in the formula.

3. Click the **Enter** button. The result, 85200, takes the place of the formula you entered in cell B15, and the formula remains visible in the formula bar, as shown in Figure 2-6.

4. Repeat steps 1-3 to enter similar formulas into cells **C15**, **D15**, and **E15**, substituting C, D, and E respectively for the Bs used above in the formula's cell addresses.

5. Click cell **A17** to activate it and enter the label **Profit** into the cell. Profit is the result of Income, or Sales, minus Total Expenses.

6. Click cell **B17** and enter the formula **=B9-B15** into the cell, then press [**Tab**]. Excel subtracts Quarter 1 Expenses from Quarter 1 Sales to arrive at 884800, the profit for Quarter 1.

7. Repeat the previous step to enter similar formulas into cells **C17**, **D17**, and **E17**, substituting C, D, and E respectively for the Bs used above in the formula's cell addresses. Your worksheet should now resemble the one shown in Figure 2-7.

8. Save your workbook.

More

As you have seen, Excel formulas use cell addresses and the arithmetical operators + for addition and – for subtraction. Since the standard computer keyboard does not contain multiplication or division symbols, the asterisk (*) is used for multiplication, and the forward slash (/) is used for division to specify the desired calculation. Using cell addresses, called cell referencing, helps Excel keep your calculations accurate by automatically recalculating results whenever the value in a cell referenced in a formula is altered.

Figure 2-6 Entering a formula

Formula displayed in
the formula bar

Results calculated
using the entered
formula

Label in A15
partially covered

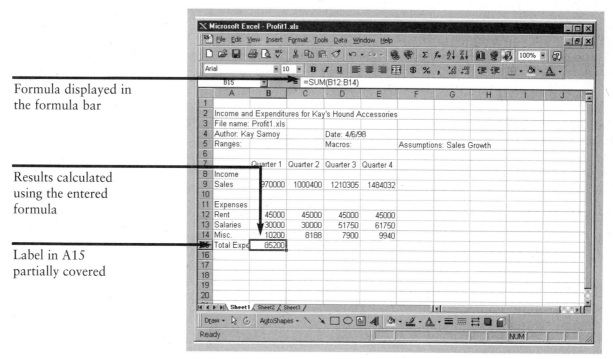

Figure 2-7 Calculating total expenses and profit

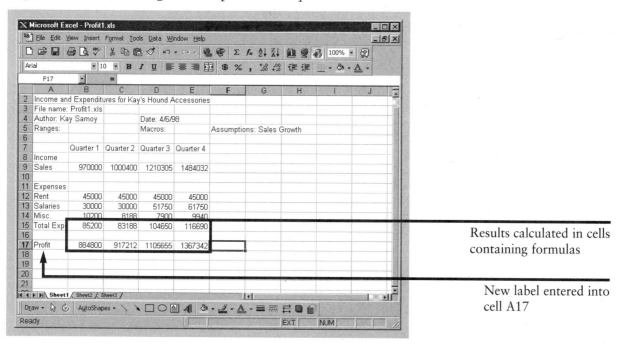

Results calculated in cells
containing formulas

New label entered into
cell A17

Practice

To practice entering formulas, follow the instructions on the **Prac2-3** tab of the practice file **MyPractice 2.xls**.

Hot Tip

If you select two or more cells that contain values, their sum will appear in the status bar. Right-clicking the sum in the status bar will open a pop-up menu that allows you to select other forms of tabulation.

Using Functions

Concept

Instead of having to create a new formula each time you want to perform a simple calculation in a worksheet, you can use one of Excel's predefined formulas, called **functions**. Excel has hundreds of these built-in formulas, covering many of the most common types of calculations performed by spreadsheets.

Do It!

Kay wants to use the SUM function to calculate her Total Expenses.

1 Click cell **B15** to make it active.

2 Press [**Delete**] to clear the previously entered formula. The data disappears, allowing the contents of cell A15 to be visible.

3 Click the **AutoSum** button $\boxed{\Sigma}$. The AutoSum function automatically sets up the formula for adding together the values directly above the active cell. The sum formula (=SUM B12:B14) appears in cell B15 and in the formula bar. The cells being added, called the argument, are indicated with an animated border. (See Figure 2-8.) The sum formula contains the notation B12:B14, called a range, which refers to all cells between B12 and B14.

4 Press [**Enter**] to confirm Excel's assumption and apply the formula to the worksheet. The value 85200 appears in the cell.

5 Click cell **F7**, then enter the label **Total for Year**.

6 Click cell **F9** to make it the active cell.

7 Click the **AutoSum** button $\boxed{\Sigma}$. The SUM function appears in the cell followed by the correct range B9:E9. Since there are no values above the active cell, AutoSum uses the values in the cells to the left of the cell pointer.

8 Click the **Enter** button. The value 4664737 now appears in the cell, as shown in Figure 2-9.

9 Save your worksheet.

More

In the example above, you used the AutoSum button to enter the SUM function into cell B15 in place of the formula =B9+C9+D9+E9. But, unlike AutoSum, most Excel functions require the user to manually enter additional information after the function name. This information, enclosed in parentheses and called the **argument**, can be cell references or other data which the function needs to produce a result. The function acts upon the argument, as the SUM function above acted on the range of cells enclosed in the parentheses that followed it.

Figure 2-8 Using the AutoSum function

6					
7		Quarter 1	Quarter 2	Quarter 3	Quarter 4
8	Income				
9	Sales	970000	1000400	1210305	1484032
10					
11	Expenses				
12	Rent	45000	45000	45000	45000
13	Salaries	30000	30000	51750	61750
14	Misc.	10200	8188	7900	9940
15	Total Expe	=SUM(B12:B14)		104650	116690
16					
17	Profit	970000	917212	1105655	1367342
18					

Animated border indicating the argument of the formula

SUM formula

Figure 2-9 Calculating the total expenses for the year

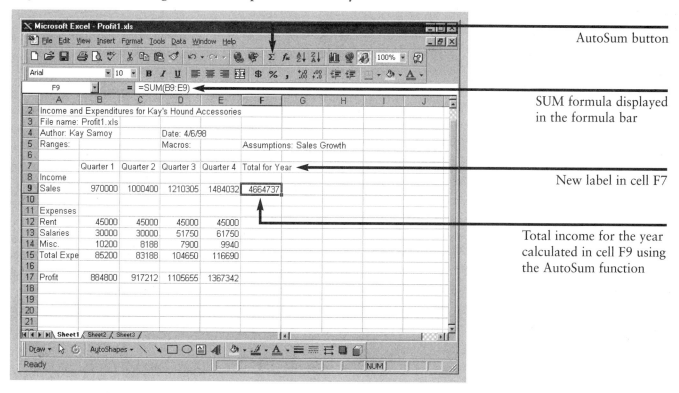

AutoSum button

SUM formula displayed in the formula bar

New label in cell F7

Total income for the year calculated in cell F9 using the AutoSum function

 # Using the Paste Function Feature

Concept

To enter a function other than SUM, you can either enter it yourself or use the **Paste Function** command.

Do It!

Kay would like to use the Paste Function command to calculate the average total quarterly expenses for the year.

1 Click cell **B19** to activate it.

2 Click **Insert**, then click **Function**. The Paste Function dialog box will open (Figure 2-10), and an equals sign will appear in the selected cell indicating that a formula is to follow.

3 Click **AVERAGE** in the Function name box to select it. A description of what the AVERAGE function does will appear below the function category and name boxes.

4 Click `OK`. The Paste Function dialog box will disappear, and the Formula Palette will appear with the range B17:B18 listed as the argument in the Number1 text box. Since this is not the correct range of cells, a new range must be specified as the argument.

5 To select the range for the total expenses, click cell **B15**, then drag to cell **E15**. An animated border will appear around the selected cells, and as you drag, the Edit Formula dialog box will reduce itself to the Number1 text box displaying the selected range. When you release the mouse button, the Formula Palette will reappear in full and the formula =AVERAGE (B15:E15) will appear in the formula bar and in cell B19, as shown in Figure 2-11.

6 Click `OK`. The Formula Palette closes and cell B19 will display the result 97432.

7 Click cell **A19**, then label it **Ave. Exp.** Your worksheet should now resemble the one shown in Figure 2-12.

8 Save your worksheet.

More

When the Paste Function dialog box appears, the default setting for the function category is Most Recently Used. If you have not used the Paste Function command before, this category contains a default list of commonly used functions. Each function on this list can also be found under a more specific category. To find other functions, you can select other categories by clicking on them. The list of Function Names changes to correspond to the category you have chosen.

You may have noticed that the title of the upper text box on the Formula Palette, Number1, is in bold face whereas the title of the text box beneath it is not. The bold title indicates that data must be entered in the box in order for the function to work. Plain text indicates that entering text is optional.

Figure 2-10 Paste Function dialog box

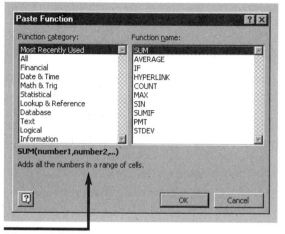

Name and
description of
the selected
function

Figure 2-11 Selecting an argument for a function

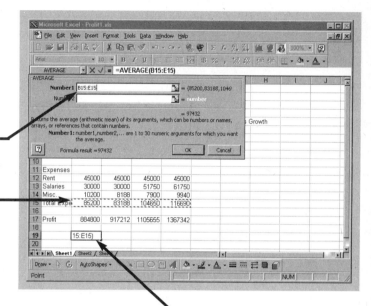

Range of the selected
argument

Dotted outline delineates
selected range

Formula is entered into the
active cell with the selected
range inserted as the argument

Figure 2-12 Pasted function

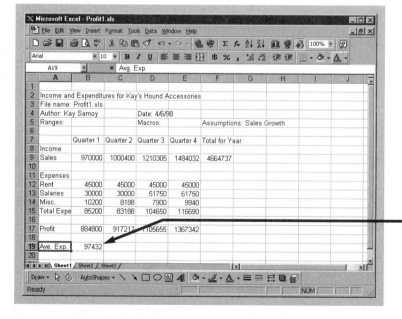

Result of the pasted function

Practice

To practice inserting functions, follow the
instructions on the **Prac2-5** tab of the practice file **MyPractice 2.xls**.

Hot Tip

Instead of using the mouse to select an
argument for a function in the Formula
Palette, you can enter a range of cells
using the keyboard.

Copying and Pasting Formulas

Concept

Formulas can be copied and pasted into other cells just as you would with values or labels. Unless instructed otherwise, Excel considers the cell referred to in an argument to be a **relative cell address**. This means that if you copy a formula or function into another cell, Excel will substitute new cell references that are in the same position relative to the new formula or function location.

Do It!

To calculate the annual totals for her various expenses, Kay will copy the SUM function from cell F9 and paste it into cells F12, F13, F14, and F15.

1 Click cell **F9** to activate it. The SUM function appears in the formula bar with the argument B9:E9.

2 Click the **Copy** button 📋 to copy the formula to the Windows Clipboard. An animated border appears around cell F9.

3 Click cell **F12** to select it.

4 Click the **Paste** button 📋 to insert the copied function into the active cell. The result 180000 appears in cell F12. Notice that Excel has changed the argument in the formula bar from B9:F9 to B12:E12, the range of cell addresses relative to the copied function's position in the worksheet, so that the function will be applied to the row it is in rather than the one it was copied from.

5 Click the fill handle of the cell pointer surrounding cell **F12** and drag down to cell **F15**. A gray border, shown in Figure 2-13, will appear around the range as you drag to indicate the target cells.

6 Release the mouse button. The SUM formula will be copied into cells F13, F14, and F15. Check your results against those in Figure 2-14.

7 Save the workbook as **Profit1.xls**.

More

Using relative cell references is similar to giving directions that explain where to go from the present location. Relative cell references follow the same directional instructions regardless of your starting position, such as "the four cells to the left of" or "the three cells above." In the preceding example, the formula told Excel to calculate the average of the values in the four cells to the left of the cell containing the formula. Wherever that formula is pasted, Excel will examine the four cells to the left of the target cell for values. Any cells that are blank, or do not contain values (such as those with labels), will be included in the calculation as zero. If you had attempted to paste the AVERAGE formula used above into a cell in column B, there would not be enough cells to the left of the target cell to fulfill the required argument, and the error message #REF! would have appeared in the cell.

Figure 2-13 Copying a formula using the fill handle

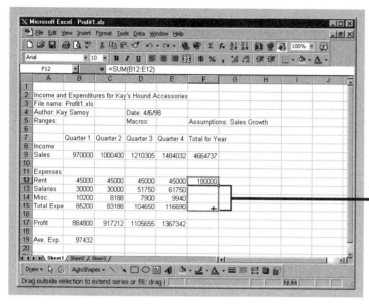

Formula will be pasted into these cells when the fill handle is released

Figure 2-14 Results of copied formula

10						
11	Expenses					
12	Rent	45000	45000	45000	45000	180000
13	Salaries	30000	30000	51750	61750	173500
14	Misc.	10200	8188	7900	9940	36228
15	Total Expe	85200	83188	104650	116690	389728
16						
17	Profit	884800	917212	1105655	1367342	
18						

Practice

To practice copying and pasting formulas, follow the instructions on the **Prac2-6** tab of the practice file **MyPractice 2.xls**.

Hot Tip

You can select the characteristics of a cell's information that you wish to paste by using the Paste Special command found on the Edit menu.

Using What-If Analysis

Concept

Excel makes it easy for you to change certain conditions of your worksheet, allowing you to see how these changes would affect the results of various spreadsheet calculations. This is called **what-if analysis,** and is one of Excel's most useful features.

Do It!

Kay wants to see what her sales would have been in Quarters 2, 3, and 4, assuming they grew 10% from the amount shown for the first quarter ($970,000).

1 Select the contents of cells **C9, D9,** and **E9.** These are the sales figures for the second, third, and fourth quarters and will be recalculated with the new assumption.

2 Press [Delete] to remove the values from the selected cells. Notice that the values in cells F9 and C15:E15 change. This is due to the fact Excel automatically recalculates formulas when values in their referenced cells have been altered. The values in cells C9:E9 are now considered to be zero.

3 Click cell I5 to select it.

4 Enter .1 (ten percent expressed as a decimal) into the active cell. This is the cell that will be referenced in the formula that calculates projected earnings.

5 Click cell **C9** to select it. Notice that Excel inserts a zero before the .1 in cell I5 as a place holder.

6 Now you must create a formula to multiply first quarter sales by 110%, which will show the results of a 10% increase. Enter the formula **=B9*(1+I5)** into the active cell, as shown in Figure 2-15. The dollar signs preceding the column letter I and the row number 5 tell Excel not to change the cell address, even if the formula is moved to a new location. This is known as an **absolute cell reference.**

7 Press [Enter]. The result of the calculation, 1067000, appears in place of the formula in cell C9. Cell F9 and B17 both change to reflect Excel's recalculation of their formulas, which include the cell C9 in their argument.

Figure 2-15 Using absolute cell references to perform what-if analysis

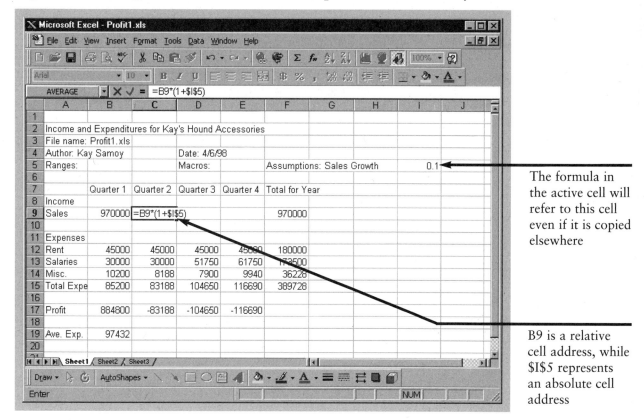

The formula in the active cell will refer to this cell even if it is copied elsewhere

B9 is a relative cell address, while I5 represents an absolute cell address

Using What-If Analysis (continued)

Do It!

8 Click the **Copy** button [icon] to copy the cell's formula to the Clipboard. A animated border appears around cell C9 to indicate that the selection is ready to be copied.

9 Click cell **D9** to activate it, then click the **Paste** button [icon]. The pasted formula appears in the formula bar and the result, 1173700, appears in the cell. Notice that the reference to cell B9 has changed to C9, but that the reference to cell I5 remains the same. If the dollar signs had not been included, the copied formula would have replaced the cell reference I5 with J5, an empty cell, and the result would have been wrong.

10 Click cell **E9** to activate it, then click the **Paste** button [icon]. As before, the formula is pasted and a new result, 1291070, appears in the cell, as shown in Figure 2-16.

11 Press [**Enter**] to confirm that the correct formula has been pasted into the target cell.

12 Click the **Save** button [icon] to save your work.

More

Formulas can contain several **operations**. An operation is a single mathematical step in solving an equation, such as adding two numbers or calculating an exponent. When working with formulas that contain multiple operators, such as 12/200+4*8, Excel performs the calculations in the following order:

1. Exponents
2. Multiplication and division, from left to right
3. Addition and subtraction, from left to right

Operations inside parentheses are calculated first, in accordance with the rules above. For example, in the calculation 12/200+4*8, the operations would be performed as follows: first, 12 would be divided by 200, then four would be multiplied by 8, and finally the two results would be added together. If the equation was 12/(200+4)*8, then the operations would be calculated like this: first, 200 would be added to 4, then 12 would be divided by the result, and finally the dividend would be multiplied by 8.

Figure 2-16 Copying a formula containing an absolute cell address

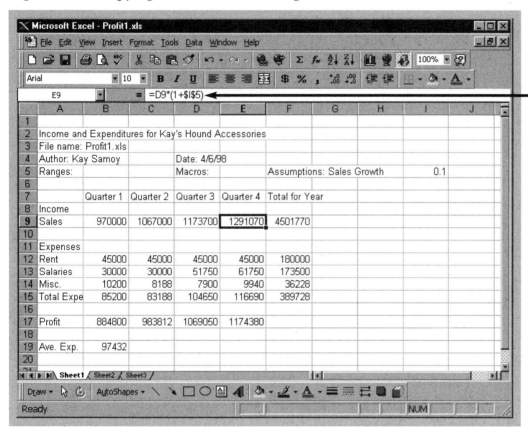

Though the relative cell address changed from B9 to D9 when the formula was copied, the absolute address for cell I5 remains unchanged

Printing
a Worksheet

Concept

Printing your worksheet is useful if you would like to have a paper copy to file, reference, or send to others. Excel allows you view the worksheet as it will appear on the printed page before it is printed so that you can spot errors or changes you would like to make before going through the printing process.

Do It!

Kay will display her worksheet in print preview mode, then print it.

1. Make sure your computer is properly connected to a working printer. (Ask your instructor.)

2. Click the **Print Preview** button ▣ on the Standard toolbar. The worksheet will be displayed in Print Preview mode, as shown in Figure 2-17. The mouse pointer appears as a magnifying glass 🔍.

3. Click at the top of the preview page. The worksheet will be magnified so that you can examine it more closely, and the pointer will change to an arrow. Since gridlines are non-printing items, they do not appear in the preview.

4. Click Print... on the Print Preview toolbar. The view will revert to regular mode and the Print dialog box, Figure 2-18, will open.

5. Click OK . The Print dialog box will close, a box will appear notifying you of the print job's progress, and the document will be sent to the printer.

More

You can adjust many printing options by selecting the Page Setup command on the File menu. The Page Setup dialog box will open with four tabs: Page, Margins, Header/Footer, and Sheet. The **Page** tab controls the way in which the printed selection will appear on the page, such as its horizontal or vertical orientation, or by how much or how little it is magnified. The **Margins** tab allows you to adjust the amount of space between printed matter and the edges of the page. The **Header/Footer** tab allows you to enter items that will appear at the top or bottom of each page, such as page numbers, titles, file names, or the name of the author. The **Sheet** tab lets you select how your data is presented on the printed page, such as whether or not you want to print gridlines, which parts of the worksheet you want to print, and whether you want column heading to be repeated across each new page.

Figure 2-17 Previewing your worksheet

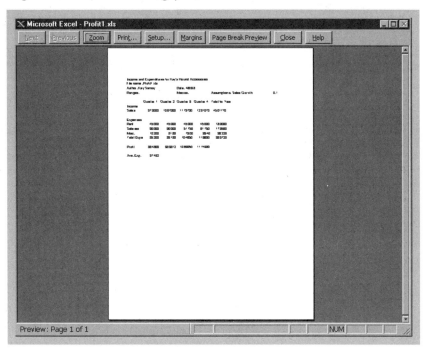

Figure 2-18 Print dialog box

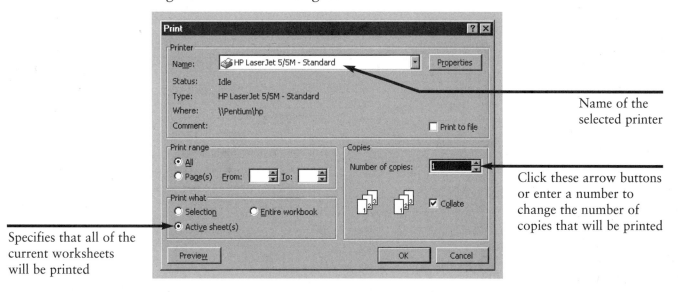

Name of the selected printer

Click these arrow buttons or enter a number to change the number of copies that will be printed

Specifies that all of the current worksheets will be printed

Practice

To practice previewing and printing worksheets, follow the instructions on the **Prac2-8** tab of the practice file **MyPractice 2.xls**.

Hot Tip

If you do not need to conduct a print preview or adjust the settings in the Print dialog box, you can print the active worksheet by clicking the Print button 🖨 on the Standard toolbar.

Shortcuts

Function	Button/Mouse	Menu	Keyboard
Copy data to the Clipboard	📋	Click Edit, then click Copy	[Ctrl]+[C]
Cut data to the Clipboard	✂	Click Edit, then click Cut	[Ctrl]+[X]
Paste data from the Clipboard	📋	Click Edit, then click Paste	[Ctrl]+[V]
AutoSum	Σ		
Paste Function	fₓ	Click Insert, then click Function	
Print Preview	🔍	Click File, then click Print Preview	
Print	🖨 (to skip Print dialog box)	Click File, then click Print (for Print dialog box)	[Ctrl]+[P] (for Print dialog box)

Identify Key Features

Figure 2-19 Identify items on the Excel screen

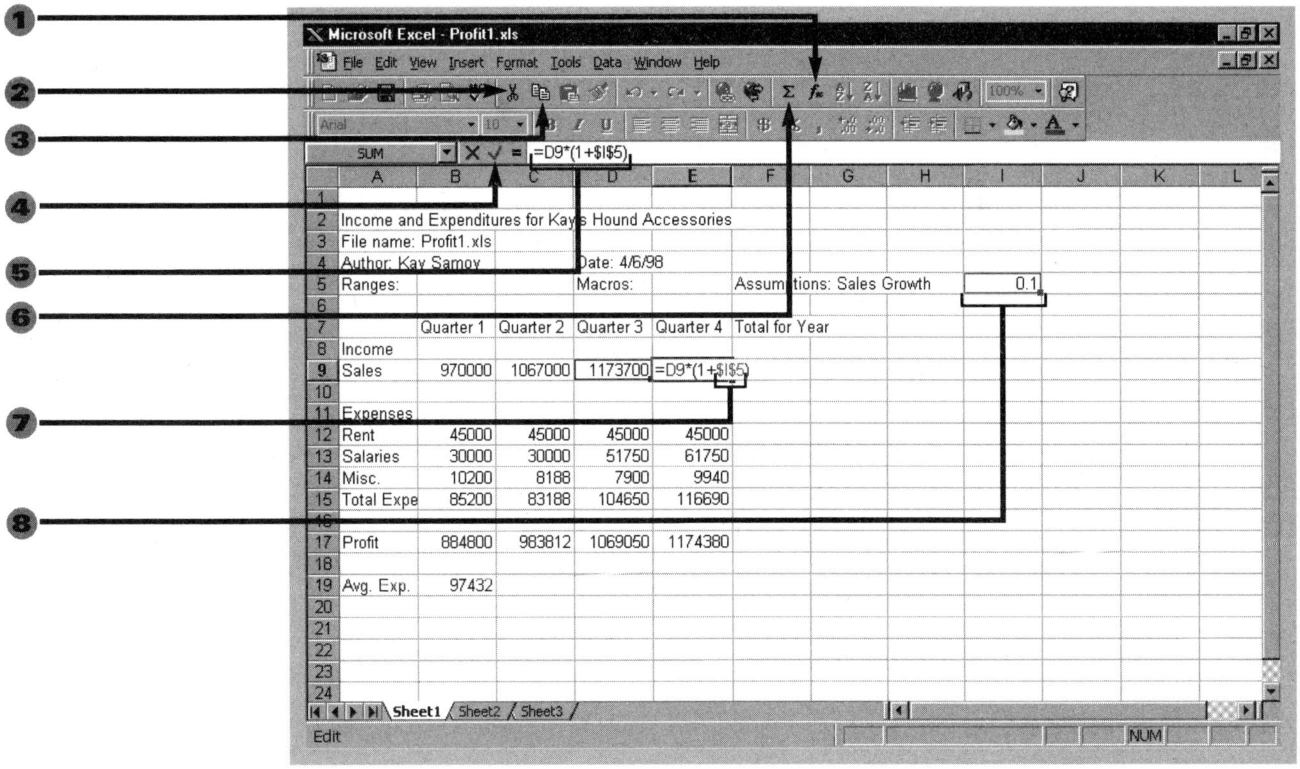

Select the Best Answer

9. The small square in the lower right corner of the active cell

10. A temporary storage space for cut or copied information

11. Use this symbol to represent multiplication in a formula

12. Allows you to view a worksheet as it will appear on an actual page

13. Lets you adjust margins or switch the page orientation

14. Offers **AVERAGE** as one of its choices

a. Page Setup dialog box

b. Print Preview

c. Paste Function dialog box

d. Asterisk

e. Fill handle

f. Clipboard

Quiz (continued)

Complete the Statement

15. When using the Fill handle, cells to be filled are indicated by a:

    a. ScreenTip

    b. Plus sign

    c. Check mark

    d. Gray border

16. Typing an apostrophe before a number instructs Excel to recognize it as a:

    a. Label

    b. Value

    c. Function

    d. Formula

17. All of the following actions will erase the Clipboard except:

    a. Pasting an item

    b. Cutting a new item

    c. Copying a new item

    d. Turning off the computer

18. By default, Excel considers referenced cell addresses to be:

    a. Absolute

    b. Copied from the Clipboard

    c. Relative

    d. AutoSums

19. Changing conditions to see how the results affect spreadsheet calculations is called:

    a. Absolute analysis

    b. Variable analysis

    c. Assumption analysis

    d. What-if analysis

20. An animated border indicates that the cell contents:

    a. Will be deleted

    b. Are the result of a function or formula

    c. Have been sent to the Clipboard

    d. Have been pasted

Interactivity

Test Your Skills

1. Enter values into your spreadsheet:

   a. Open the file you created in the first lesson, **Test 1.xls**.

   b. Fill in values to display how many hours you spend on each activity every day. For example, if you have four hours of class on Monday, enter the number 4 in the cell where the Monday column intersects with the Class row.

   c. If any of the values are repeated during the week, use the Copy and Paste commands to copy them from one cell to the others.

2. Use the AutoSum function to total the number of hours you spend on each activity during the week.

   a. Create a **Total Hours** label in the same row as the days of the week labels, in the column directly to the right of the Sunday column.

   b. Use AutoSum to enter the total hours you spend in class in the cell where the Total Hours column and the Class row intersect.

   c. Use the fill handle to copy the AutoSum function into the next five cells in the Total Hours column in order to calculate the total hours for the remaining daily activities.

3. Calculate the average time you spend on each activity each week by using the Paste Function command:

   a. Enter the label **Average** in the cell directly to the right of Total Hours.

   b. Select the cell where the Average column intersects with the Class row. Then use the Paste Function command to place the average number of hours spent in class during the week in the active cell.

   c. Place the averages for the five other daily activities in the Average column by using the Fill handle.

4. Preview and print the worksheet:

   a. Switch to Print Preview mode.

   b. Zoom in on the right side of the worksheet.

   c. Change the orientation of the page to Landscape.

   d. Print the worksheet.

   e. Return to normal view and save the file as **Test 2.xls**.

Interactivity (continued)

Problem Solving

Using the skills you have learned so far, create a spreadsheet that will allow you to track your individual monthly expenses for a year. Divide the year into four quarters, and use category labels such as rent, phone bill, books, food, entertainment, etc. Calculate your total expenses for each quarter, as well as your average quarterly expenses. Also include an assumption value of five percent to account for going over your allotted budget. Then conduct a what-if analysis to recalculate your total and average expenses based on a five percent increase in one of the categories. Save the file as **Solved 2.xls**.

L E S S O N

3

FORMATTING WORKSHEET ELEMENTS

As you work with your spreadsheet, you will find that you use certain groups of cells that contain related data repeatedly. Excel allows you to define these groups as ranges, and name them as you see fit. Then, rather then select the range by dragging the mouse over it, you can select the appropriate cells quickly and accurately with the name box.

Formatting refers to changing the appearance of information in a worksheet without changing its actual content. You can use Excel's many formatting tools to improve the appearance and the effectiveness of your spreadsheet. Text formatting includes font, font size, style, color, and alignment. Labels can also be formatted in a variety of styles, some of which help to express the kind of data they represent. You can format individual cells or ranges of cells. The AutoFormat command permits you to apply a set of predesigned formats to an entire range at once.

Although the structure of an Excel spreadsheet is highly organized, it is also very flexible. You can change the structure by increasing or decreasing column widths and row heights. You can also add and delete rows and columns as necessary. Changes to the structure of your worksheet depend on the data it contains and the formatting you have applied.

Case Study:
Kay will continue to develop and organize her spreadsheet by naming her ranges and adding formatting to her data. She will also modify the physical structure of the worksheet in order to improve its layout.

Defining and Naming Ranges

Concept

A **range** is any group of two or more cells, usually contiguous. The range B12 to E12 consists of these two cells, called **anchor cells**, and all cells between them. The data for this range is Kay's rent. Range addresses are defined by citing the first and last cell in the range separated by a colon. The address for the range for Kay's rent is B12:E12. Ranges are named so that they are easy to locate. These names can also be used in formulas.

Do It!

Kay wants to define and name all of the ranges in her worksheet that contain data.

1 Click cell **B9**, then drag to cell **F9** to select these cells. The range for Sales is defined as B9:F9, and will be highlighted.

2 Click the **Name** box [B9   ▾]. The cell name B9 will become active, indicated by its highlighting.

3 Type **Sales**, then press [**Enter**]. The range B9:F9 is now named Sales, and the range name will appear in the Name box whenever cells B9 to F9 are selected.

4 Repeat this process to name the remaining row labels, being sure to press [**Enter**] after each range name. Name the range **B12:E12 Rent**, the range **B13:E13 Salaries**, the range **B14:E14 Miscellaneous**, the range **B15:E15 Total_Expenses**, and the range **B17:E17 Profit**. Be sure to include the underscore ([Shift]+[-]) in the name Total_Expenses, because range names cannot contain any spaces. When you click the Name box drop-down arrow, your name box list should now resemble the one shown in Figure 3-1.

Figure 3-1 Defining and naming ranges

Named ranges listed
alphabetically in the
Name box drop-
down list

The range B17:E17
is named Profit

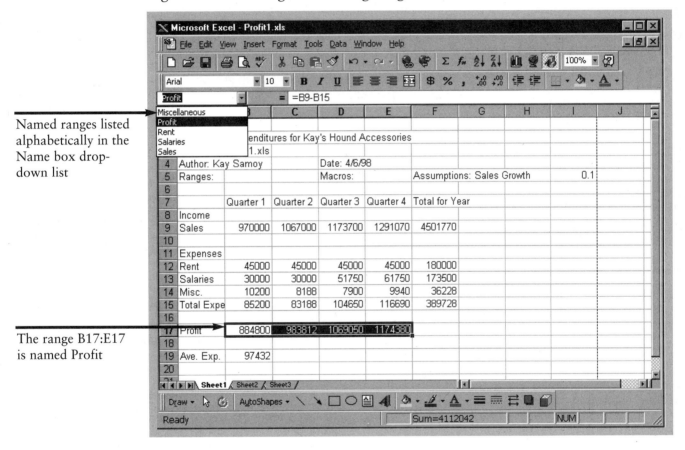

Defining and Naming Ranges (continued)

Do It!

5 Click cell **B8**, and drag down to cell **B17**. The range B8:B17 will be selected.

6 Click **Insert**, highlight **Name**, then click **Define**. The Define Name dialog box, shown in Figure 3-2, will open with the range name Quarter_1 in the Names in Workbook text box. Excel automatically picks up a column or row label as the default range name if it is adjacent to, or included in, the range selected. You can change this name if you wish, but we will use the defaults for this exercise.

7 Click ⬚ OK ⬚ to name the range.

8 Click cell **C8**, then hold [**Shift**] down and click cell **C17**. The range C8:C17 will become highlighted. Holding the shift key down highlights all of the cells between the first and the last cells you select.

9 Repeat step six to name this range **Quarter_2**.

10 Use the Define Name dialog box to name the range **D8:D17 Quarter_3**, the range **E8:E17 Quarter_4**, and the range **F8:F17 Total_for_Year**.

11 Click elsewhere in the worksheet to deselect the range.

12 Click the **Save** button 🖫 to save the changes you have made to the worksheet.

More

Ranges do not have to made up of cells that are touching. They can contain nonadjacent blocks of cells, or multiple nonadjoining cells. To create a nonadjacent range, highlight the first group of cells or a single cell that you wish to include, then hold down [Ctrl] while selecting the next cluster of cells. You can select as many non-contiguous cells or ranges as you desire. Clicking anywhere else in the worksheet will deselect the ranges.

Figure 3-2 Define Name dialog box

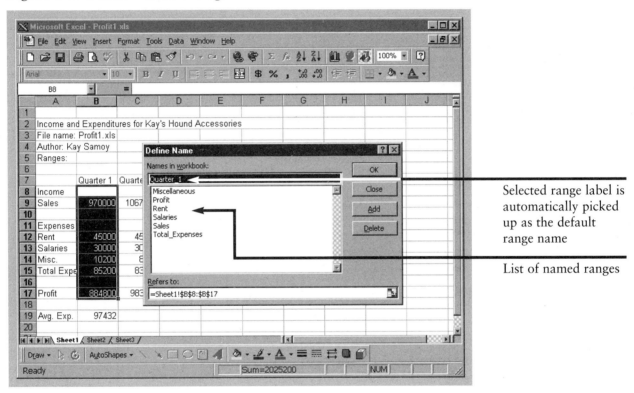

Selected range label is automatically picked up as the default range name

List of named ranges

Practice

Open the practice file **Practice–Lesson 3.xls,** save it as **MyPractice3,** and then follow the instructions on the **Prac3-1** tab.

Hot Tip

Use the Name list box to quickly select a range to be used in a formula or to be formatted.

Formatting Cell Contents

Concept

Formatting enhances the appearance of your worksheet and can make your labels stand out, so they will be easier to read. Formatting options include changing the font (typeface and size), style, and alignment of your text. A cell or range must be selected before formatting can be applied.

Do It!

Kay wants to add formatting to various cells to emphasize their contribution to the worksheet.

1 Click the **Name** box drop-down arrow, then click **Profit** on the list of named ranges that appears. If Profit had not been visible, you would have had to use the scroll bar on the right edge of the list to access the rest of the range names it contains.

2 Click **Format**, then click **Cells**. The Format Cells dialog box will open.

3 Click the **Font** tab to bring it to the front of the stack, as shown in Figure 3-3.

4 Notice that the current font (Arial), font style (regular), and size (10 point) are highlighted. From the Font Style list, select **Bold**. The letters in the Preview box will be made bold so that you may view the results of this change before you apply it.

5 Click [OK]. The dialog box will close and the numbers contained in the range named Profit will appear bold, as shown in Figure 3-4.

6 Click cell **A2** to make it active.

7 Click the **Font** box drop-down arrow. A list of the fonts installed on your computer will appear.

8 Drag the scroll bar box on the Font list down until **Times New Roman** is visible, then move the pointer over Times New Roman and click. The typeface of "Income and Expenditures for Kay's Hound Accessories" will change from Arial to Times New Roman.

9 Click the **Font Size** text box. The current point size of 10 will become highlighted, ready to be changed.

10 Type **14**, then press [Enter]. The title will increase in size.

11 Select the range **A2:K2**. These are the columns across which the title will be centered.

12 Click the **Merge and Center** button 🔳, then click elsewhere on the worksheet to deselect the columns. Figure 3-5 shows the new title placement.

Figure 3-3 Format Cells dialog box

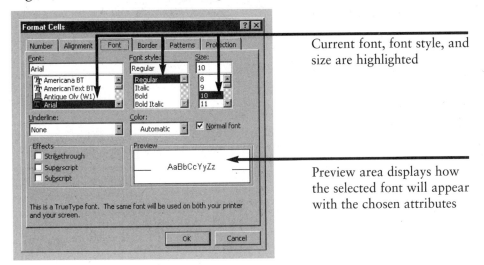

Current font, font style, and size are highlighted

Preview area displays how the selected font will appear with the chosen attributes

Figure 3-4 Bolding cell data

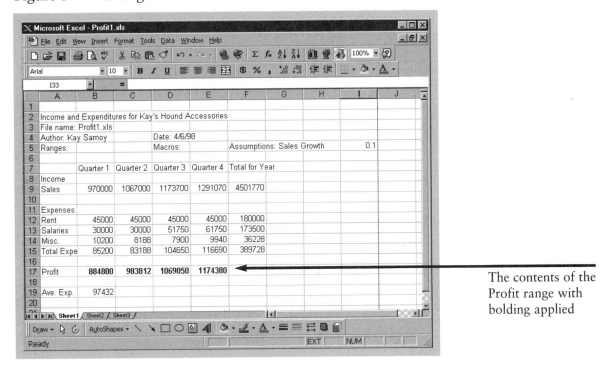

The contents of the Profit range with bolding applied

Figure 3-5 Formatted worksheet title

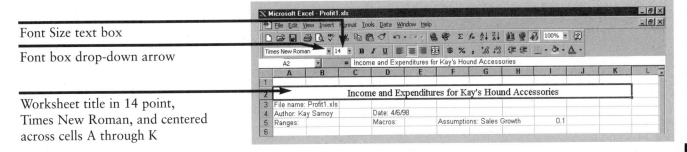

Font Size text box

Font box drop-down arrow

Worksheet title in 14 point, Times New Roman, and centered across cells A through K

Formatting Cell Contents (continued)

Do It!

13 Select the range **B7:F7**.

14 Click the **Italics** button I. The column labels will change to italicized type.

15 Click the **Underline** button U. Each column label will be underlined. Notice that the Italic and Underline buttons are indented. An indented button indicates that a particular formatting option is being applied.

16 Select the range **A8:A19**.

17 Click the right edge, the arrow, of the **Font Color** button $\underline{A}$. The Font Color palette, shown in Figure 3-6, will open.

18 Select the blue color box in the second row of the palette, then click anywhere on the worksheet to deselect the range. The row labels will change to blue. Your worksheet should appear as the one shown in Figure 3-7.

19 Click **File**, then click **Save** to save your work.

More

The **Font** tab in the Format Cells dialog box allows you to change most of the attributes relating to text. The options Font, Font style, and Size each have two boxes attached to them. The lower box is a list box that indexes available fonts, font styles, and font sizes respectively. The upper box is a text box wherein you can enter any of these choices without having to scroll through the list. However, the point size of your font selection is not limited to only those numbers listed, and can be anywhere between 1 and 409.

The **Underline** option contains a drop-down list with five styles of underlines that can be used. The **Color** option contains a drop-down palette with 56 color choices. Clicking one of these boxes will turn your text that color. Checking the **Normal Font** box reverts any changed font formats to the default settings described above. There are three effects you can select: **Strikethrough** draws a line through text, making it appear as if it has been crossed out; **Superscript** shrinks the text and raises it above the baseline; **Subscript** shrinks and drops the text below the baseline. Any alteration to a font formatting characteristic that you make will appear in the preview window in the tab, and none of the changes made will take effect on the worksheet until the OK button is clicked.

Figure 3-6 Font Color palette

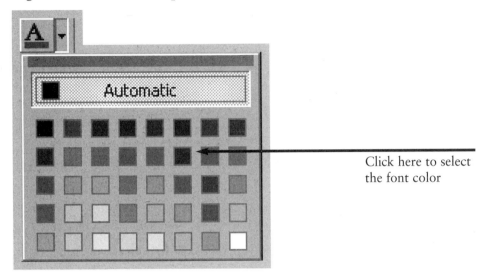

Click here to select
the font color

Figure 3-7 Formatted cell contents

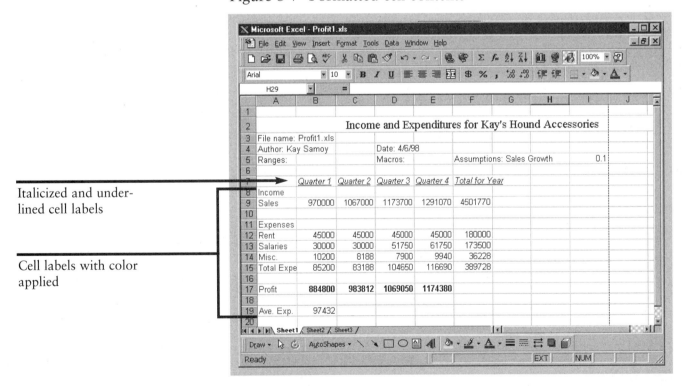

Italicized and under-
lined cell labels

Cell labels with color
applied

Practice

To practice formatting cell labels, follow the
instructions on the **Prac3-2** tab of the practice file **MyPractice3.xls**.

Hot Tip

Clicking an indented formatting button
removes the applied format and reverts the
button to its normal, flat, state.

Working with Rows and Columns

Concept

There are times when the information you enter into your worksheet will not fit neatly into a cell set with the default height and width. Therefore you may need to adjust the height of a row or, more commonly, the width of a column. The standard column width is 8.43 characters, but can be set anywhere between 0 and 255.

Do It!

Kay wants to widen some of the columns in her worksheet to accommodate long labels and values.

1 Move the mouse pointer onto the dividing line between the column A and column B heading buttons. The pointer will change from a cross ⊹ to a double-arrow ↔ that will allow you to resize the column.

2 Click and hold the left mouse button. The gridline that divides the columns will become dotted and the column width will appear in a ScreenTip.

3 With the mouse button depressed, drag the column boundary to the right until the width reaches **13.00** characters. The entire label "Total Expenses" will be visible. While the "Total Expenses" label was cropped before you resized the column, notice that the label in cell F7, Total for Year, is fully visible. Excel will display a label that is longer than its cell is wide in its entirety as long as the cell it intrudes upon is empty.

4 Click the column B heading button to select the entire column. Notice that cell A2 also becomes selected since it has been merged with cells B2:K2, and therefore when one these cells is selected the entire merged area, now a single cell, will become active.

5 While holding [**Ctrl**], click the column C, D, E, and F heading buttons so that all five columns are selected, as shown in Figure 3-8.

6 Click **Format**, highlight **Column**, then select **Width** from the submenu. The Column Width dialog box, Figure 3-9, will open.

7 Type **14** in the Column Width text box, then click ▭ OK ▭. Columns B through F will increase in width to 14 characters. This width is to accommodate formatting that you will apply to the cell data in a later skill.

8 Save your work.

More

You can also adjust the height of the rows in your worksheet. Row height is measured in points, just as fonts are, and there are 72 points per inch. Dragging the line between two row heading buttons is one way to change a row's height. There is a Row command on the Format menu that allows you to alter height as well. Row height usually does not need to be changed manually, because Excel will adjust row height to fit the largest point size of a cell's label or data.

Table 3-1   Column Formatting Commands

COMMAND	FUNCTION
Width	Adjust the width to a specified number of characters
AutoFit Selection	Adjust the width to fit the widest cell entry
Hide	Hides a selected column from view
Unhide	Displays a hidden column
Standard Width	Allows you to set a default width size, and resets selected columns to the specified size

Figure 3-8 Selecting columns to be resized

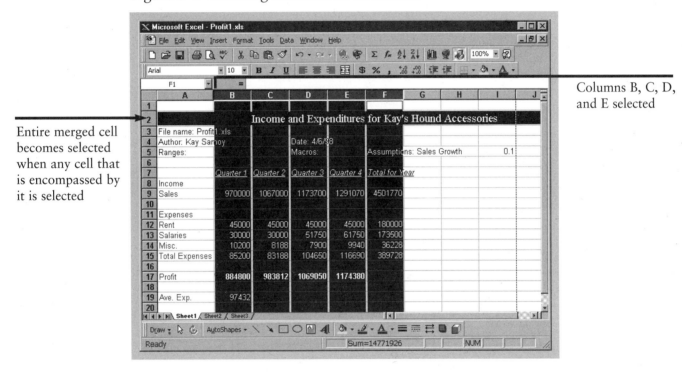

Entire merged cell
becomes selected
when any cell that
is encompassed by
it is selected

Columns B, C, D,
and E selected

Figure 3-9 Column Width dialog box

Practice

To practice working with column and row widths, follow the instructions on the **Prac3-3** tab of the practice file **MyPractice3.xls**.

Hot Tip

You can automatically resize a column's width to fit the widest entry by double-clicking the right edge of the column heading button.

Skill

Inserting and Deleting Rows and Columns

Concept

In Excel you can add and delete columns or rows to customize your worksheet to your specific needs. For example, you may want to add another column for new inventory products, or perhaps even delete a row that contains expenses that are no longer current.

Do It!

Kay wants to add an additional row between her documentation sections and the main body of her worksheet, and she wants to remove the column between Assumptions and the assumption value.

1. Click cell **A6** to make it active.

2. Click **Insert**, then click the **Cells** command. The Insert dialog box, Figure 3-10, will open with the Shift cells down radio button selected.

3. Click the **Entire row** radio button. This tells Excel to add a row and shift all of the rows below row 6 down.

4. Click ⬚OK⬚. A new row will be inserted, the contents of the worksheet will shift down by one row, and your formulas will be updated to reflect the row shift.

5. Click cell **H5** to make it active.

6. Click **Edit**, the click **Delete**. The Delete dialog box, similar to Insert, will open with the Shift cells left radio button selected.

7. Click the **Entire column** radio button, then click ⬚OK⬚. Cell H5 will be deleted and the Sales Growth data will move from I5 to H5. Even though the Sales values for Quarters 2 through 4 are based on the absolute address of the assumption, Excel will recalculate the formulas based on the new cell address. Compare your worksheet with that of Figure 3-11.

8. Save your workbook.

More

A **dummy column** or **dummy row** is a blank column or row included at the end of a defined range that is used to hold a place or create blank space. A dummy row between a range of values and a cell containing a formula to average them allows Excel to include the added row in the range rather than considering it to be an unrelated value. Then, if a row or column is added to the original range, Excel will recalculate any formulas that include that range to include the change. If you need to add a row or column to a range that does not include a dummy, you must manually adjust your formulas to take into account the new cells and values. If a row or column is inserted into the middle of an existing range Excel is able to recalculate any formulas that reference that range. It is only when you need to add a row or column to the end of an existing range that is being used in a formula that a dummy row or column becomes necessary.

Figure 3-10 Insert dialog box

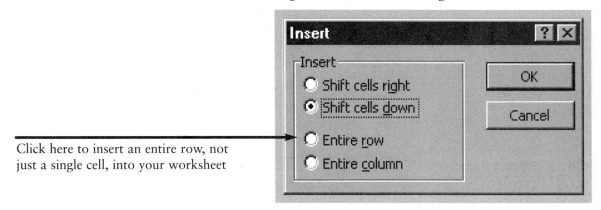

Click here to insert an entire row, not
just a single cell, into your worksheet

Figure 3-11 Worksheet with an inserted row and a deleted cell

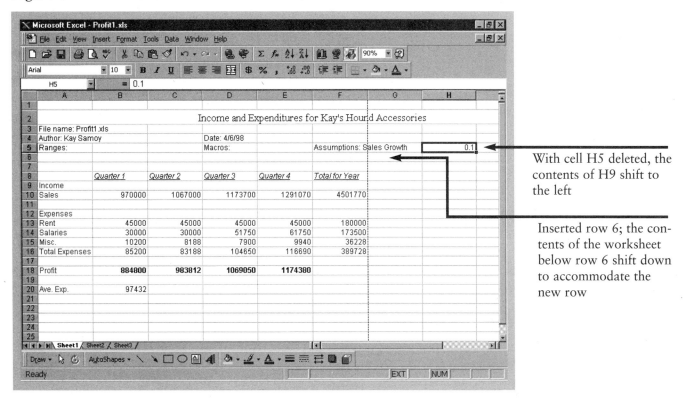

With cell H5 deleted, the
contents of H9 shift to
the left

Inserted row 6; the con-
tents of the worksheet
below row 6 shift down
to accommodate the
new row

Practice

To practice inserting and deleting rows and
columns, follow the instructions on the
Prac3-4 tab of the practice file
MyPractice3.xls.

Hot Tip

Right-clicking (clicking the right mouse
button) brings up various pop-up menus.
Where you right-click in the Excel window
will determine which pop-up menu
appears. Try right-clicking various elements
of the Excel window to view these menus.

Formatting Cell Values

Concept

Although labels can help identify what kind of data a number represents, you may want to format the values themselves so that their function is more apparent. Common formats include **Currency**, **Percentage**, **Fraction**, and **Comma**. The format you choose will depend on how the values are to be used, and how you want them to appear. Cell or range formatting can be applied before or after data is entered.

Do It!

Kay wants to format all of her values with commas so that they will be easier to read, format the Profit range in Currency style, format her assumption in Percentage style, and then decrease the number of decimal places in cell B20.

1. Select the range **B10:F20**.

2. Click the **Comma Style** button , . All of the cells contained within the selected range will be formatted in the comma style, which includes two decimal places.

3. Click the **Name box** drop-down list arrow, then click **Profit** on the list of ranges that appears. The range B18:F18 will be highlighted.

4. Click the **Currency Style** button $. The values entered in the Profit row will appear with dollar signs preceding them and two decimal places to represent cents.

5. Click cell **H5** to make it the active cell.

6. Click the **Percentage Style** button % . The originally entered value of 0.1 will appear as 10%. The result of the formula whose argument references this cell will remain the same.

7. Click cell **B20** to activate it.

8. Click the **Decrease Decimal** button ·00 ·0 twice. The two decimal places will be erased. Figure 3-12 displays the worksheet as it should now appear.

9. Save the worksheet.

More

When you applied the Currency, Comma, and Percentage styles to the worksheet, you used the default settings for each of these buttons. The **Number** tab of the Format Cells dialog box, shown in Figure 3-13, can be accessed by selecting the Cells command on the Format menu. It allows you to apply one of twelve different formatting styles to cells. Most of the categories of formatting listed on the Numbers tab can be customized to suit the specific needs of your worksheet and personal preferences.

The number of decimal places values are taken and the appearance of date and time references can be altered, special formats can be defined for use in databases, and custom number formats can be created for advanced users of Excel.

Figure 3-12 Cell values with formatting applied

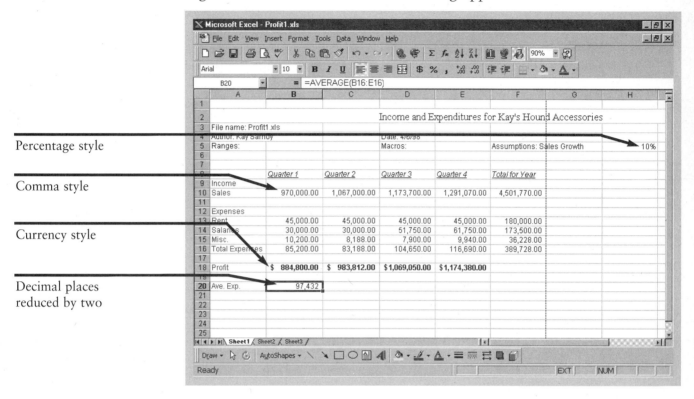

Percentage style

Comma style

Currency style

Decimal places
reduced by two

Figure 3-13 Format Cells dialog box

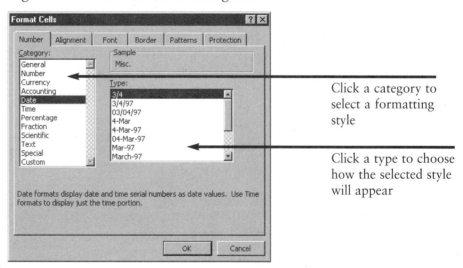

Click a category to
select a formatting
style

Click a type to choose
how the selected style
will appear

Practice

To practice formatting cell values, follow
the instructions on the **Prac3-5** tab of the
practice file **MyPractice3.xls**.

Hot Tip

If a cell is too narrow to display a value
correctly, Excel will display number signs
(######) in place of the data, though the
actual value is unaffected. Making the cell
wide enough to properly accommodate the
data will make it reappear correctly.

Using AutoFormat

Concept

The **AutoFormat** command allows you to add one of sixteen sets of formatting to selected ranges, creating tables that are easy to read and visually stimulating. Numbers, borders, fonts, patterns, alignment, and the height and width of rows and columns can all be altered using the AutoFormat options. AutoFormat alters the appearance of tables using colors, fonts, and textures.

Do It!

Kay wants to use the AutoFormat function to improve the appearance of her worksheet and to set the main body data off from the documentation.

1 Select the range **A8:F20** to make this area active.

2 Click **Format**, then select the **AutoFormat** command. The AutoFormat dialog box, shown in Figure 3-14, will open.

3 Drag the **Table Format** list box scroll bar down to reveal the lower portion of the Table format list, then select **3D Effects 2**. The Sample box will change to reflect the appearance of the chosen format.

4 Click `OK`, then click anywhere in the worksheet to deselect the area. The range A8:F20 will appear as shown in Figure 3-15.

5 Select the range **A3:H5** to make this group of cells active.

6 Click **Format**, then select **AutoFormat** to open the AutoFormat dialog box.

7 Select **List 1** from the Table format list, then click the **Options** button `Options >>`. The AutoFormat dialog box will grow to display six format types that you can include or exclude when the AutoFormat is applied.

8 Click **Font, Width/Height,** and **Alignment** so they do not display a check in their check boxes. The Sample table will show how the range will look with these options off. These options were turned off so as to preserve the font, size, and placement of the title, and the width of the columns.

9 Click `OK`, then click anywhere in the worksheet to deselect the range. Figure 3-16 shows the worksheet documentation with AutoFormatting.

10 Save your workbook.

More

Colors and borders can be added to single cells, specific rows or columns, and non-adjacent ranges by using the Color 🎨▾ and Borders buttons ▦▾. The Color button allows you to fill a cell or range with a color selected from the Color palette. One of twelve borders can be used to accentuate or differentiate cells.

Figure 3-14 AutoFormat dialog box

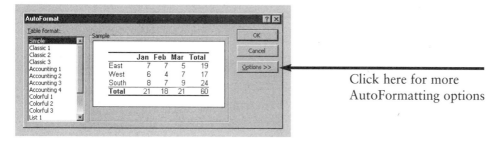

Click here for more
AutoFormatting options

Figure 3-15 AutoFormatting applied to the selected range

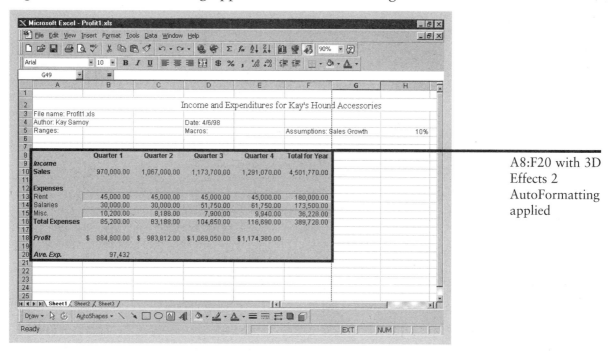

A8:F20 with 3D
Effects 2
AutoFormatting
applied

Figure 3-16 List 1 AutoFormatting applied

A3:H5 with List 1 AutoFormatting
applied with the font, width/height,
and alignment of kept intact.

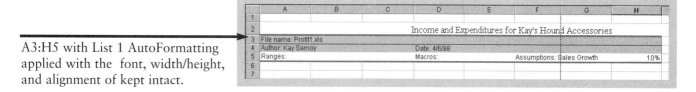

Practice

To practice using AutoFormat, follow the instructions on the **Prac3-6** tab of the practice file **MyPractice3.xls**.

Hot Tip

The None option on the Table Format list in the AutoFormat dialog box will return a range to its original, unformatted, style.

Filling a Range with Labels

Concept

Excel can automatically fill a range with several types of series information. Series information includes numbers, numbers combined with text (such as Quarter 1), dates, and times. Excel can step a series by a constant set value, or multiply by a constant factor. The way a series fills will depend on the type of value and the incremental setting.

Do It!

To explore the AutoFill feature, Kay wants to erase the Quarter column headings and then replace them.

1 Click cell **B8** to select it, then press the **[Backspace]** key to delete the cell label.

2 Repeat this process for cells **C8**, **D8**, and **E8**. The range B8:E8 will be empty.

3 Click cell **B8**, then type **Quarter 1**.

4 Move the mouse pointer to the fill handle of the cell pointer surrounding cell **B8**. It will change to the crosshairs.

5 Drag the pointer to cell **E8**. As you drag the pointer, a dimmed border will appear indicating the cells that have been selected, and ScreenTips will appear showing what will be placed in the cell where the mouse pointer currently is, as shown in Figure 3-17.

6 Release the mouse button. The range B8:E8 will be filled with Quarter 1 through Quarter 4.

7 Close your workbook, but do not save these changes, as deleting and reentering cell information removes AutoFormatting

More

In the above example, you used **AutoFill** to enter a series of labels into a range of cells. Along with AutoFill, there are three other series fill types that you can use: Linear, Growth, and Date. These are advanced options and are found in the **Series** dialog box, shown in Figure 3-18, which can be accessed by clicking the Edit menu, selecting Fill, then clicking Series from the submenu.

A **Linear** series fill, with the Trend box unchecked, adds the Step Value to the value in the cell selected. With Trend checked, the Step Value is disregarded and the trend is calculated based on the average of the difference between the values in the selected cells. This average is then used to fill the range by increasing or decreasing the value by a constant amount. If necessary, the original selected cell information is replaced to fit the trend.

A **Growth** series fill is similar to a linear series fill, except that instead of adding values together, numbers are multiplied to create a geometric growth trend. A series created based upon dates uses the options in the Date Units list. You can extend selected dates by day, weekday, month, or year. The Stop Value can be set so as to fix a value at which the series will end. If the selected range is filled before it reaches the Stop Value, it will end at that point.

Figure 3-17 Filling a range with labels

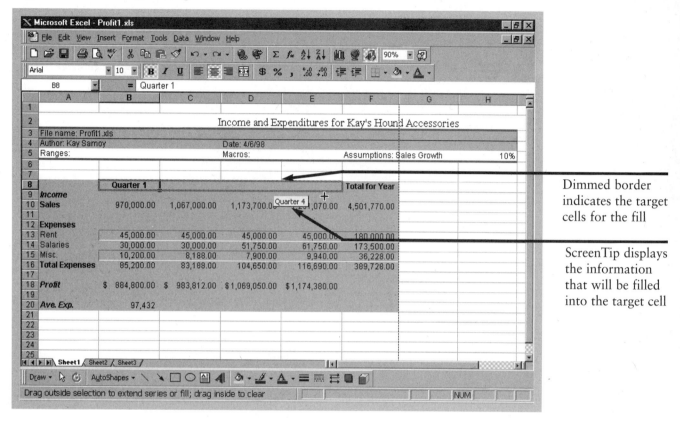

Dimmed border indicates the target cells for the fill

ScreenTip displays the information that will be filled into the target cell

Figure 3-18 Series dialog box

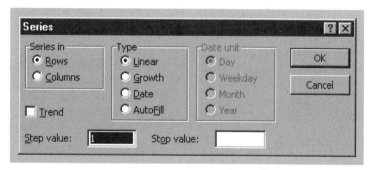

Practice

To practice filing ranges with labels, follow the instructions on the **Prac3-7** tab of the practice file **MyPractice3.xls**.

Hot Tip

If you select a value, then hold the right mouse button while dragging the fill handle, a pop-up menu will appear allowing you to choose the type of series that is inserted into the destination cells.

Shortcuts

Function	Button/Mouse	Menu	Keyboard
Merge cells and center contents	▦		
Merge cells		Click Format, then click Cells, then click Alignment	[Ctrl]+[1]
Make a label bold	B	Click Format, then click Cells, then click Font	[Ctrl]+[B]
Italicize a label	I	Click Format, then click Cells, then click Font	[Ctrl]+[I]
Underline a label	U	Click Format, then click Cells, then click Font	[Ctrl]+[U]
Add color to a label	A ▾	Click Format, then click Cells, then click Font	[Ctrl]+[1]
Comma style	,	Click Format, then click Style	
Currency style	$	Click Format, then click Style	
Percent style	%	Click Format, then click Style	
Increase or decrease decimal places	+.0 or .00		

Identify Key Features

Figure 3-19 Identify the formatting components of the Excel screen

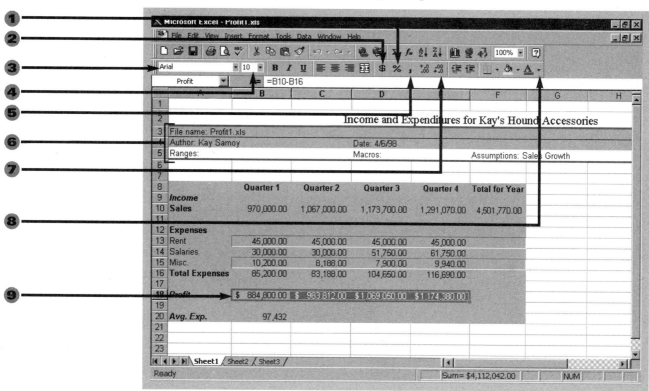

Select the Best Answer

10. Allows you to select a named range quickly and accurately

11. Contains a tab with options for changing font, font style, and font size

12. Combines the contents of multiple cells into one cell

13. Lets you add a set of predetermined formatting options to a spreadsheet

14. Contains the Bold, Italic, and Underline buttons

a. Merge and Center button

b. Formatting toolbar

c. Name box

d. Format Cells dialog box

e. AutoFormat command

Quiz (continued)

Complete the Statement

15. All of the following are effects available on the Font tab of the Format Cells dialog box except:

    a. Strikethrough

    b. Strikescript

    c. Superscript

    d. Subscript

16. An appropriate way to express a range address is:

    a. B9/E9

    b. B9;E9

    c. B9-E9

    d. B9:E9

17. A range name may not contain:

    a. Uppercase letters

    b. Labels used in the spreadsheet

    c. Spaces

    d. Numbers

18. The Formatting toolbar offers all of the following formatting styles except:

    a. Currency style

    b. Percent style

    c. Fraction style

    d. Comma style

19. The standard width of a worksheet column is:

    a. 8.43 characters

    b. 13.00 characters

    c. 13.5 characters

    d. 255 characters

20. All of the following can be done from the Insert menu except:

    a. Insert a blank row

    b. Insert a blank column

    c. Define and name a range

    d. Apply an AutoFormat

Interactivity

Test Your Skills

1. Define and name the ranges in a spreadsheet:

   a. Open the file **Test 2.xls** that you created at the end of the previous lesson.

   b. Define and name the following ranges using the name box: **Class, Activities, Meals, Studying/Homework, Leisure,** and **Sleep.**

   c. Define and name the following ranges by opening the Define name dialog box from the Insert menu: **Monday, Tuesday, Wednesday, Thursday, Friday, Saturday, Sunday, Total Hours,** and **Average.**

2. Format cell labels in a spreadsheet:

   a. Change the font of the title of your worksheet to **Times New Roman,** and then change its size to 12 point.

   b. Merge and center the title across the first ten columns of the worksheet.

   c. Add bold formatting to the days of the week labels. Italicize and underline the **Total Hours** and **Average** labels.

   d. Change the font color of the daily activities labels in Column A to red, and then make them bold.

3. Adjust the columns and rows in your spreadsheet:

   a. Click and drag the right border of Column A until the column is 18.00 characters wide.

   b. Click and drag the right border of the Wednesday column until the entire label "Wednesday" is visible.

   c. Double-click with the mouse to automatically resize the **Total Hours** column so that its label fits.

   d. Add an extra row between the documentation and data sections of your worksheet.

4. Add advanced formatting to your spreadsheet:

   a. Reduce all values in the Average column to three decimal places.

   b. Apply **Comma style** to all values in the Total Hours column.

   c. Apply the AutoFormat **3D Effects 1** to the documentation section of the worksheet.

   d. Apply the AutoFormat **Classic 3** to the data section of your worksheet, but preserve the font and width/height that the worksheet already has.

   e. Save the file as **Test 3.xls.**

Interactivity (continued)

Problem Solving

Utilize the knowledge and skills you have acquired about spreadsheet design to keep yourself on track as you work toward earning a diploma. Using Excel, create a worksheet that displays your graduation requirements and the means by which you are fulfilling them. Include courses you may have already taken, your current courses, and the courses you will need and would like to take in the future. Also include data such as the total number of credits you need to graduate and the percentage you have so far. Calculate how many credits you will need to average each academic semester. Then see if your actual numbers are on pace. Finally, be sure to take advantage of Excel's formatting features to enhance the organization and appearance of your spreadsheet. Save the file as **Solved 3.xls**

L E S S O N

INSERTING OBJECTS AND CHARTS

Though the labels and values you enter into a spreadsheet serve as its core, other objects may represent certain data better or simply illustrate it further. Inserting these objects can break up the monotony of row after row of numbers and allow you to explain or highlight aspects of your spreadsheet that might otherwise go unnoticed.

You can insert a number of objects into your worksheet for the purpose of annotating specific information. These include text boxes, shapes such as arrows and connectors, and comments. Text boxes can be any size, but will obscure the portions of the worksheet behind them. Comments are similar to text boxes, but can be hidden from view. All graphics can be formatted and manipulated in a variety of ways.

One very effective way of enhancing your worksheet visually is to add a chart. The Chart Wizard can guide you through the process of creating a graphical representation of a data series that you select from your Excel worksheet. Charts can be moved, resized, and formatted. You can even change a chart's type and characteristics after it has been created. In addition, individual chart elements can be customized for emphasis and clarity.

Case Study:
In this lesson, Kay will strengthen her spreadsheet by inserting graphics and creating a chart using the Chart Wizard. Afterward, she will use some of Excel's advanced printing features to print a new copy of her worksheet.

Inserting Text Boxes

Concept

Text can also be inserted into a worksheet within a **text box**. Creating text boxes allows you to add passages of any size and appearance without the constraints of a cell in the worksheet.

Do It!

Kay wants to insert a text box into her worksheet to emphasize the growth in projected Quarter 4 sales.

1 Click **View,** highlight **Toolbars,** then click **Drawing** if it is not already checked. The Drawing toolbar will be visible.

2 Click the **Text Box** button 🖼. The pointer will change to the text cursor ↓ when it is in the workspace, which allows you to create a text box.

3 Click in cell **E6,** just below the green line where you want the top right corner of the text box to appear, then drag down and to the right to cell **F7,** until the box you have created is approximately one cell long by two cells high, like the one shown in Figure 4-1. When you release the mouse button, the borders of the box will become dotted and eight small squares called sizing handles will appear. There will be a sizing handle at each corner and one in the center of each side of the text box. A blinking insertion point will also appear in the text box.

4 Type **Up 33% from Quarter 1** to enter it into the text box.

5 Click elsewhere in the worksheet to deselect the text box. Your worksheet should now resemble the one shown in Figure 4-2.

6 Save your worksheet.

More

The primary advantage of using text boxes is their flexibility. Text boxes can be easily moved, resized, or reformatted, without affecting the appearance or content of any other part of the worksheet. When text is being entered, a text box acts as a small word-processing window. If there is not enough room on a line to fit a word, the text will **wrap** and continue on the next line. If the text box you have made is not large enough to accommodate the text as you are entering it, then the text will scroll upward, without changing the size or location of the box, to allow the additional text to be entered. The text box will have to be enlarged manually to view all of the text it contains. This can be accomplished through he use of the sizing handles, by clicking and dragging the handle in the desired direction of movement, expanding or reducing the size of the box.

Once a text box has been created, it is not fixed in place, but can be moved anywhere on the worksheet. To move a text box to another part of the worksheet, click the frame of a selected text box (not on a sizing handle) to select its frame, and then drag the text box to the desired destination.

Figure 4-1 Creating a text box

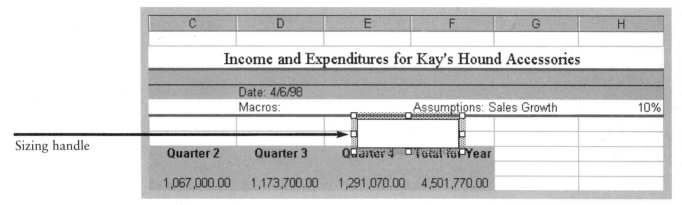

Sizing handle

Figure 4-2 Text box with text

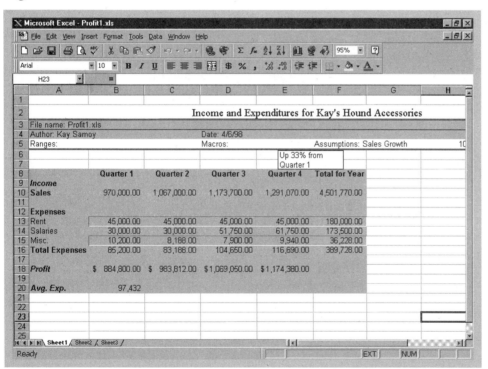

Practice

To practice inserting text boxes, open the practice file **Practice–Lesson 4.xls**, save the file as **MyPractice 4.xls**, then follow the instructions on the **Prac4-1** tab.

Hot Tip

Text boxes are always visible, and hide the portion of the worksheet behind them. Text boxes can overlap each other, however, and their order can be changed by right clicking one and choosing an option from the Order submenu that appears.

Enhancing Graphics

Concept

Graphic objects that you have inserted, such as lines, text boxes, or pictures, can be modified to alter and improve their appearance.

Do It!

Kay will add arrows and color to the text box that was inserted in the previous skill.

1 Click the **Arrow** button on the Drawing toolbar. It will indent, and the mouse pointer will appear as a thin cross + when it is over the worksheet.

2 Position the pointer just after the **1** in the text box, then click and drag to cell **E10**, the Sales value for Quarter 4. When the mouse button is released, the line that was being drawn becomes fixed, and an arrowhead appears at the end.

3 Click the text box to select it. Its frame becomes a thick hatched line.

4 Click the text box's frame (but not a sizing handle) to select the frame. It changes from a hatched to a dotted border.

5 Click the arrow on the **Fill Color** button on the Drawing toolbar to open the Fill Color palette.

6 Click the pale blue square in the bottom row of the palette to select it. The text box's background will change to match the selected color.

7 Click the arrow you drew to select it. A sizing handle appears at each end of the arrow to indicate its selection.

8 Click the **Line Color** drop-down arrow to open the Line Color palette, and select the red square in the middle of the first column. The arrow will change to match the color of the selected square.

9 Click elsewhere in the worksheet to deselect the arrow. The text box and arrow should now resemble the ones shown in Figure 4-3.

More

The Format menu is **context sensitive**, which means that its content changes based on the item that is selected. When a cell is active, the Format menu contains commands for altering a cell, while a selected AutoShape will cause another set of commands to appear on the Format menu. Objects that are inserted into an Excel document, such as lines, AutoShapes, and clip art, all have their own formatting dialog boxes with tabs relating to the selected object.

The **Format Text Box** command, available on the Format menu when a text box is selected, opens the Format Text Box dialog box shown in Figure 4-4. This dialog box contains seven tabs with options for altering many aspects of a text box. While many of the controls found in the Format Text Box dialog box have toolbar buttons, the dialog box allows more precise and comprehensive control over such aspects the size of the text box, the internal margins of the text box, and the orientation of text within a text box.

Figure 4-3 Enhancing worksheet graphics

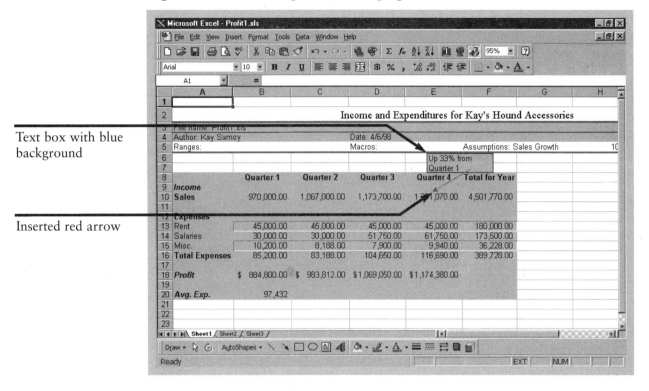

Text box with blue
background

Inserted red arrow

Figure 4-4 Format Text Box dialog box

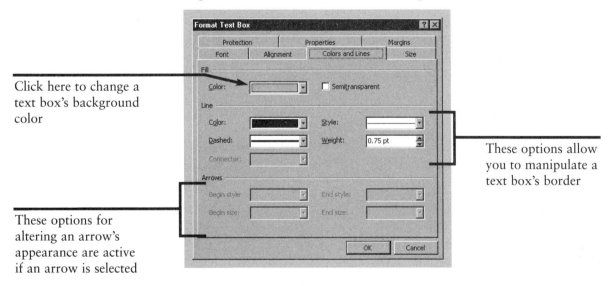

Click here to change a
text box's background
color

These options allow
you to manipulate a
text box's border

These options for
altering an arrow's
appearance are active
if an arrow is selected

Practice

To practice enhancing graphics follow the
instructions on the **Prac4-2** tab of the practice file **MyPractice 4.xls**.

Hot Tip

You can open an object's formatting dialog
box by double-clicking it. Double-clicking a
text box's frame will open the dialog box
shown above, but double-clicking in the
text box will only allow you to alter the text
itself.

Adding Comments

Concept

A **comment** is an electronic note that can be attached to a cell. Comments are hidden from view until the mouse pointer is over a cell that contains a comment. Comments are useful for documenting information or making notes. If multiple people will be using a spreadsheet, comments can be used as a way to share additional information.

Do It!

Since there is not enough room in the documentation section of her worksheet to list all of the named ranges, Kay will insert a comment containing the range names.

1 Click cell **A5** to make it active.

2 Click **Insert**, then click **Comment**. An active text box with the name of the designated user and an insertion point, shown in Figure 4-5, will appear next to the selected cell. The text box will have an arrow pointing to the cell it references and a red triangle will appear in the upper right corner of the cell indicating that it contains a comment.

3 Select the contents of the cell by dragging the I-beam over the text in the box.

4 Type **Kay Samoy:** and then press [**Enter**]. This is to indicate that Kay is the author of the comment. Notice that the name that first appeared in the comment box appears in the status bar. This can be changed from the General tab of the Options dialog box available on the Tools menu.

5 Type the following range names, pressing [**Enter**] after each: **Miscellaneous, Profit, Quarter 1, Quarter 2, Quarter 3, Quarter 4, Rent, Salaries, Sales, Total Expenses**. The text will scroll as you type, hiding the first few entries.

6 Drag the midpoint sizing handle of the bottom edge of the comment box down until it is approximately even with row 13. When you release the mouse button the comment box will expand so that all the text will be visible as shown in Figure 4-6.

7 Click elsewhere in the worksheet to deselect cell A5 and hide the comment.

8 Position the pointer over cell **A5**. The comment will be displayed.

9 Save your workbook.

More

Like cells and text boxes, comment boxes and the text they contain can be formatted. Right-clicking a cell that contains a comment opens a pop-up menu with a command for editing and deleting comments. These commands activate the comment connected to the selected cell. Double-clicking the comment's border will open the Format Comment dialog box, and clicking in the comment box will allow you to manipulate the text itself. The **Reviewing** toolbar, whose buttons are listed in Table 4-1, contains commands for displaying and navigating between comments. It can be found on the Toolbars submenu of the View menu. Once a comment has been opened for editing, you can move it anywhere in the worksheet by clicking and dragging its border; a line will always run from the comment to its parent cell.

Figure 4-5 Adding a comment to a cell

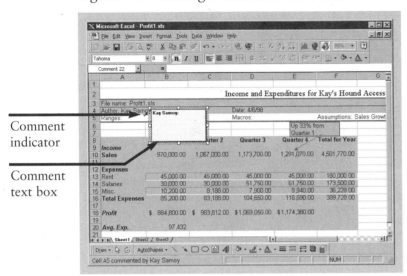

Comment
indicator

Comment
text box

Figure 4-6 Final
appearance of Kay's comment

Kay Samoy:
Miscellaneous
Profit
Quarter 1
Quarter 2
Quarter 3
Quarter 4
Rent
Salaries
Sales
Total Expenses

Table 4-1   Reviewing Toolbar Buttons

BUTTON	NAME	FUNCTION
	New Comment	Opens a new comment
	Edit Comment	Displays the comment with an insertion point in the comment pane
	Previous Comment	Displays the previous comment
	Next Comment	Displays the next comment
	Show/Hide Comment	Leaves a comment visible even when the mouse pointer is not over the selected parent cell; deselecting this button returns the comment to its default hidden state
	Show/Hide All Comments	Shows or hides all comments on the worksheet
	Delete Comment	Permanently removes a comment and its reference mark in the parent cell

Practice

To practice adding comments, follow the instructions on the **Prac4-3** tab of the practice file **MyPractice 4.xls**.

Hot Tip

Either the New Comment button or the Edit Comment button will appear on the Reviewing toolbar, depending on whether or not the selected cell already contains a comment.

Creating a Chart

Concept

Charts are graphics that represent values and their relationships. Using charts you can quickly identify trends in data, and see the contrasts among values. Excel allows you to easily portray data using a variety of two- and three-dimensional chart styles.

Do It!

Kay wants to show the values for Rent, Salaries, and Miscellaneous expenses as percentages of her total yearly expenses.

1. Select the range **F13:F15**. These are the values that are required to create the chart.

2. Click the **Chart Wizard** button on the Standard toolbar. The Chart Wizard dialog box opens, as shown in Figure 4-7, with the Column chart type selected. If the Office Assistant opens, close it by clicking its Close button, since is not necessary for this skill.

3. Click **Pie** in the Chart type list box. The Chart sub-types will change to show different type of pie charts.

4. Click Next >. The Wizard will advance to its second step with a pie chart representing the selected data displayed. If you had not already selected cells, you could enter which cells to include in your chart in the data range text box.

5. Click the **Series** tab to bring it the front of the stack.

6. Click the **Category Labels** text box to activate it. A flashing insertion point will appear in the text box so you can name the categories for your chart.

7. Click the **Collapse Dialog** button. The dialog box will shrink so only the Category Labels text box is shown. Collapsing the dialog box allows you to view more of the worksheet so you can easily select the cells to be inserted as the labels for your chart's categories.

8. Select **A13:A15**. An animated border will surround the selected range, a ScreenTip will display the size of the selection, and the range will appear in the collapsed dialog box, as shown in Figure 4-8.

Figure 4-7   Chart Wizard dialog box: Step 1

Click here to select a chart type

Name and description of the selected chart sub-type

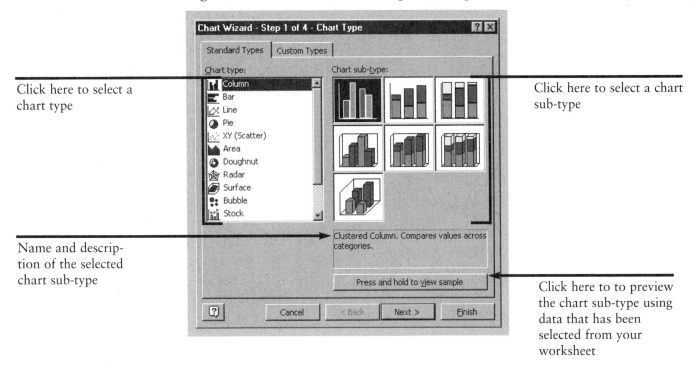

Click here to select a chart sub-type

Click here to to preview the chart sub-type using data that has been selected from your worksheet

Figure 4-8   Selecting the category labels

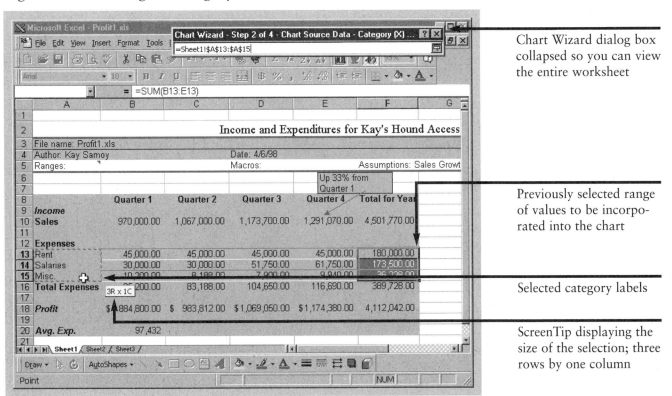

Chart Wizard dialog box collapsed so you can view the entire worksheet

Previously selected range of values to be incorporated into the chart

Selected category labels

ScreenTip displaying the size of the selection; three rows by one column

Creating a Chart (continued)

Do It!

9 Click the **Expand Dialog** button ⊡ to bring the full dialog box into view.

10 Click Next > . The third step of the wizard will be shown.

11 Click the **Chart tile** text box, then type **Breakdown of Expenses**. The title you have entered will appear in the preview area to the right of the text box. The other text boxes are grayed out since they are not applicable to the chosen chart type.

12 Click the **Legend** tab to bring it to the front of the stack.

13 Click the **Show legend** check box to deselect this option, since you will be labeling the chart later.

14 Click the **Data Labels** tab to bring it to the front of the stack.

15 Click the **Show label and percent** radio button. Labels and percentages will appear in the preview.

16 Click Next > to advance to the last step of the wizard. As you can see in Figure 4-9, the As object in radio button is selected, indicating that the chart will appear in the current worksheet.

17 Click Finish . The Chart Wizard dialog box will close, your chart will be displayed in the center of your worksheet, and the Chart toolbar will appear in the Excel window, as shown in Figure 4-10.

18 Save your workbook.

More

When the chart is selected, the Data menu is replaced by the Chart menu. The first four commands on the Chart menu open dialog boxes that are similar to the steps of the Chart Wizard. This allows you to alter any of the characteristics of the chart without having to recreate it with the Chart Wizard. The Add Data command lets you append to the ranges that are displayed.

Figure 4-9   Chart Wizard dialog box: Step 4

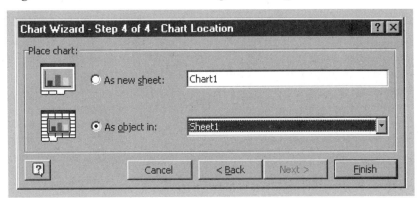

Figure 4-10   Finished chart

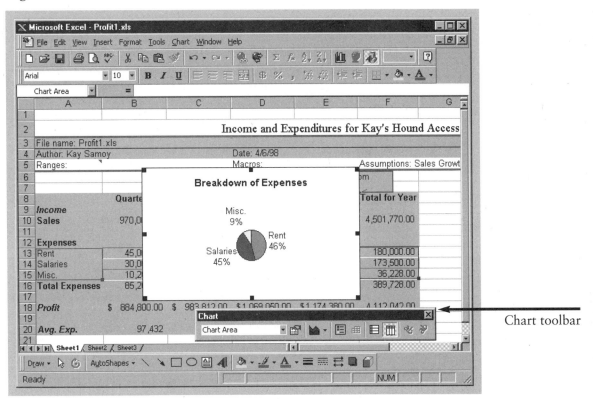

Chart toolbar

Practice

To practice creating a chart, follow the instructions on the **Prac4-4** tab of the practice file **MyPractice 4.xls**.

Hot Tip

When a chart is selected, ranges that it references will be selected in the worksheet. You can add or subtract cells from the ranges portrayed in the chart by dragging a selected range's fill handle. Moving the cell pointer selects a new range.

 # Moving and Resizing a Chart

Concept

Once you have created a chart, you can change its size and location in the work-sheet so that it complements your data without obstructing it.

Do It!

Kay wants to move the chart below the main data of her worksheet and then resize it so that its boundaries match those of existing columns and rows.

1 Click the selected chart and drag down and to the left until the upper left corner of the dotted border is in cell A21 (see Figure 4-11). As you move the mouse the pointer will change to the movement pointer ✦ and the dotted border will indicate where the chart will appear when the mouse button is released. The worksheet will scroll upward when the mouse pointer is dragged below the document window.

2 Scroll downward until the entire chart can be seen in the document window, if it is not already.

3 Position the mouse pointer over the midpoint sizing handle of the right edge of the chart, then click and drag the edge of the chart to the left until it is even with the boundary between columns C and D. The chart will adjust itself so it remains centered and proportional in its box.

4 Using the midpoint sizing handle on the bottom of the chart, drag the chart edge to the boundary between rows 34 and 35. Notice that the chart elements expand slightly to fill the larger area. Your chart should resemble the one shown in Figure 4-11.

5 Save your workbook.

More

Object Resizing Techniques

ACTION	TO
Press [Shift] while dragging the chart	Constrain a chart's movement to only the horizontal or vertical
Press [Ctrl] while dragging the chart	Copy the chart to another place in the worksheet
Press [Shift] while dragging a corner sizing handle	Constrain a chart's aspect ratio when resizing it
Press [Ctrl] while dragging a sizing handle	Maintain a chart's center point when resizing
Press [Ctrl]+[Shift] while dragging a corner sizing handle	Maintain a chart's center point and aspect ratio when resizing

Figure 4-11 Repositioned and resized chart

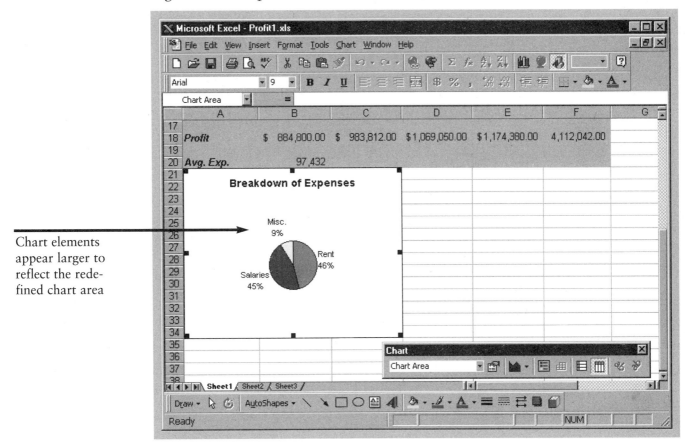

Chart elements appear larger to reflect the redefined chart area

Practice

To practice moving and resizing a chart, follow the instructions on the **Prac4-5** tab of the practice file **MyPractice 4.xls**.

Hot Tip

As you move the mouse pointer over various elements of the chart, ScreenTips will appear with a brief explanation of that item. These ScreenTips can be disabled by pressing [Alt].

99

Formatting a Chart

Concept

After a chart has been created, many of its aspects can be altered. The color and location of chart elements can be changed, and formatting can be added to text.

Do It!

Kay wants to emphasize that her company has met its goal of keeping miscellaneous expenses under 10% of total expenses; to do this, she will isolate the corresponding pie slice in the chart and change its color. She would also like to format the chart title.

1. Click the pie in your chart to make it active. Three sizing handles will appear indicating its selection.

2. Click the **Miscellaneous** pie slice to select it.

3. Click and drag the **Miscellaneous** slice away from the pie so the point of the triangle is even with the former border of the pie. Notice that the slice's label moves to accommodate the slice's new position. (See Figure 4-12.)

4. Double-click the **Miscellaneous** pie slice. The Format Data Point dialog box opens.

5. Click the **Patterns** tab, shown in Figure 4-13, to bring it to front if it is not already there.

6. In the **Area** section of the tab, click the yellow box in the bottom row, beneath the currently selected color. The sample color, shown in the lower left of the tab, will change to illustrate the newly selected color.

7. Click OK . The dialog box closes, and the chart will appear with the new color applied to the Miscellaneous slice.

8. Double-click the chart's title, **Breakdown of Expenses**, to open the Format Chart Title dialog box.

9. On the Patterns tab, click the **Shadow** check box to activate it.

10. Click OK . The dialog box closes, and the chart's title now appears in a box with a shadow applied to it. Click elsewhere in the worksheet to deselect the chart title; your chart should now resemble the one shown in Figure 4-13.

More

Double-clicking any element of a chart will open a dialog box that enables you to format and alter the selected chart element. Depending upon what item is selected, the available tabs of this dialog box will provide the appropriate formatting options. Elements can also be selected and their formatting dialog boxes opened using the Chart toolbar, shown in Figure 4-14.

On the **Patterns** tab of chart element formatting dialog boxes there is a **Fill Effects** button that lets you apply advanced formatting options such as gradients, textures, patterns, or pictures to the selected element.

Figure 4-12 Altered chart elements

Chart title formatted with a shadow

Miscellaneous slice yellow and
dragged away from the pie

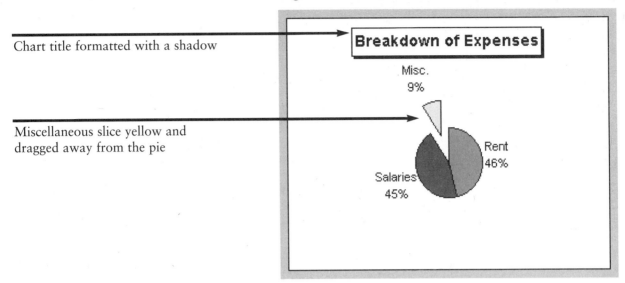

Figure 4-13 Format Data Point dialog box

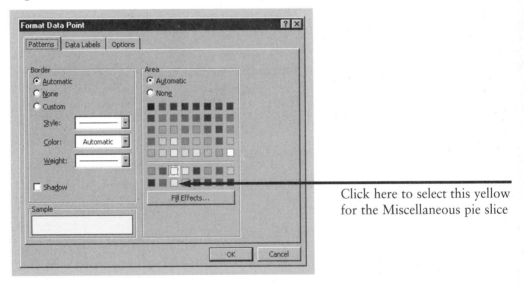

Click here to select this yellow
for the Miscellaneous pie slice

Figure 4-14 Chart toolbar

Practice

To practice formatting a chart, follow the
instructions on the **Prac4-6** tab of the practice file **MyPractice 4.xls**.

Hot Tip

Chart titles and labels can be dragged to
new locations in the chart area, as can the
chart itself.

 ## Changing a Chart's Type

Concept

Excel allows you to change a chart's **type** while maintaining the same referenced data series. For example, a bar chart can be easily converted to a line graph if it will more effectively present the data it contains. You can also switch between variants of the same chart type, called sub-types, that will make your chart easier to read.

Do It!

Kay would like to display her pie chart with a 3-D visual effect.

1 Click **Chart**, then click **Chart Type**. The Chart Type dialog box opens with the Standard Types tab in front, with the selected chart's type and sub-type selected. (If the Standard Types tab is not in front, click it now.)

2 Click the second chart sub-type, **Pie with a 3-D visual effect**. It will become highlighted, and a description of it will appear in the area beneath the chart sub-types.

3 Click [OK]. The dialog box closes, and your chart appears with the new sub-type applied, as shown in Figure 4-15.

4 Click **Chart**, then click **3-D View**. The 3-D View dialog box, shown in Figure 4-16, appears with the current elevation of 15 degrees selected.

5 Click [⬆] twice to increase the chart's elevation to 25 degrees. The chart in the preview box will pivot, illustrating the effect that the changes you are making will have on the chart.

6 Click [OK]. The dialog box closes and the chart reflects the changes that you have made, as shown in Figure 4-17.

7 Save your workbook.

More

Chart Types

CHART TYPE	DESCRIPTION	EXAMPLE
Column	Data changes over time or quantitative comparisons among items	Quarterly income projections
Bar	Similar to a column chart, but horizontal orientation places more emphasis on the X value	Individual sales performance
Line	Trends in data at fixed intervals	Tracking stock trends
Pie	The percentage each value contributes to the whole; used for a single data series	Budgets, chief exports of a country
XY (Scatter)	Comparative relationships between seemingly dissimilar data	Scientific data analysis
Surface	The range of intersections between two sets of data	Optimal fuel consumption

Figure 4-15 Pie with a 3-D visual effect

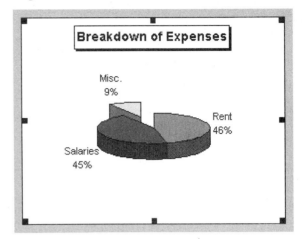

Figure 4-16 3-D View dialog box

Click here to increase
or decrease chart
elevation

Current chart elevation

Click here to rotate
chart

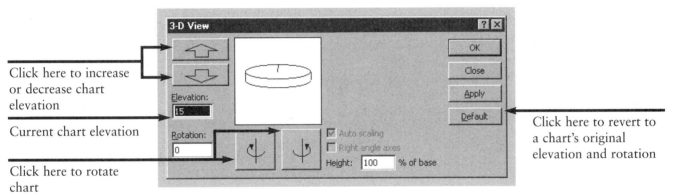

Click here to revert to
a chart's original
elevation and rotation

Figure 4-17 Chart with increased elevation

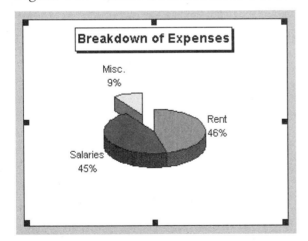

Practice

To practice changing a chart's type, follow
the instructions on the **Prac4-7** tab of
MyPractice 4.xls.

Hot Tip

The Chart Type drop-down arrow 📊 on
the Chart toolbar allows you to quickly
change the selected chart from one type to
another.

 # Using Advanced Printing Features

Concept

A worksheet, especially one such as a chart that contains embedded objects, may not always fit on a standard printed page using the default printing settings. Excel allows you preview and change page orientation so as to accommodate different arrangements of data.

Do It!

Kay wants to change the page orientation so her entire worksheet will fit onto one printed page.

1 Click outside of the chart to deselect it.

2 Click the **Print Preview** button 🔍 . Your worksheet will be displayed in Print Preview mode. Notice that the status bar reads "Preview: Page 1 of 2," and the Next button is active, indicating that there is another page.

3 Click in the upper right corner of the document preview with the magnification pointer. As you can see in Figure 4-18, the worksheet will appear magnified in the window with the worksheet title and cell labels cropped, making it apparent that the entire worksheet does not fit on the page.

4 Click Setup... . The Page Setup dialog box will appear as shown in Figure 4-19.

5 Click the **Landscape** radio button in the Orientation section of the dialog box.

6 Click OK . The dialog box will close and you will see that the entire worksheet is now visible on the preview page.

Figure 4-18 Magnified worksheet in Print Preview

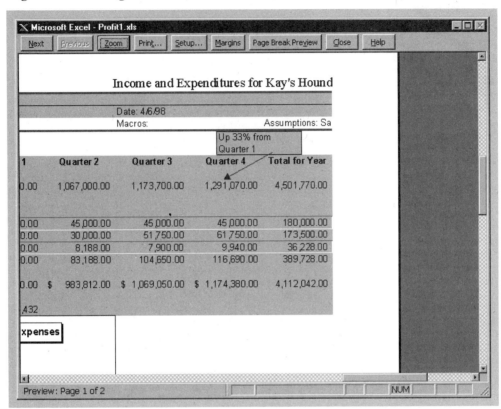

Figure 4-19 Page Setup dialog box

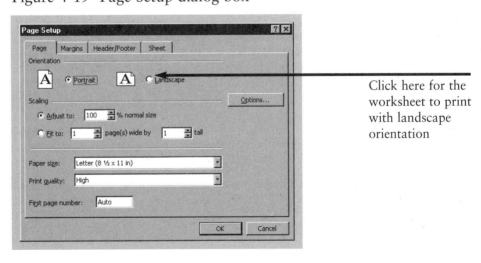

Click here for the
worksheet to print
with landscape
orientation

Using Advanced Printing Features

(continued)

Do It!

7 Click the preview to zoom out. The entire page will appear horizontally in the window but the status bar will still read Page 1 of 2, as shown in Figure 4-20.

8 Click Next . A blank page appears. This is page contains blank cells that belong to cell A2, which was merged to encompass the range A2:J2 when the title was centered. It is not necessary to print this second page since it only contains blank cells.

9 Click Print... . Print Preview will close, you will be returned to normal view, and the Print dialog box will open.

10 In the Print range section of the dialog box, click the up arrow of the **From** text box ☐⬍. A 1 will appear selected in the box, designating it as the first page to print, and the Page(s) radio button will be selected.

11 Click the up arrow in the **To** text box. A 1 will appear selected in the box, telling Excel to stop printing after page 1.

12 Click OK . The Print dialog box will close and the document will be sent to the printer.

13 Save your workbook.

More

Excel's print function allows you select the area or item you want to print. Therefore, you do not have to send an entire worksheet to the printer if you want to have a hard copy of a smaller portion. With a chart selected, the Print dialog box will have the Selected Chart radio button active in the Print what area so that only the chart, and not the remaining data of the worksheet, will be printed. Likewise, the Print Preview will display just the chart, since this view shows you exactly how the information will be printed with the current settings. If you select a chart, then click the Page Setup command found on the File menu, the Page Setup dialog box will open with a tab labeled Chart. Compare this dialog box shown in Figure 4-21 to the one shown in Figure 4-19. This tab contains options concerning the chart's printed size and print quality.

Figure 4-20 Preview of worksheet in landscape orientation

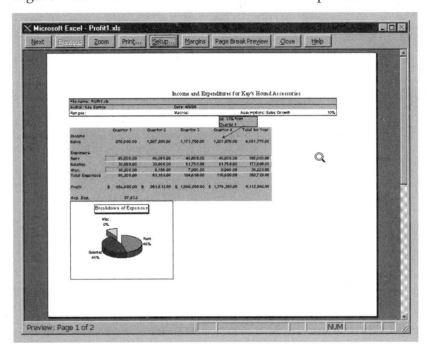

Figure 4-21 Page Setup dialog box when a chart is selected

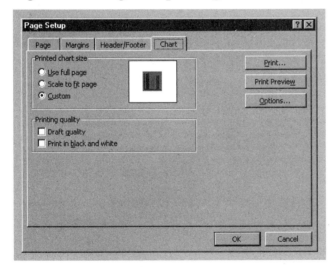

Practice

To practice using advanced printing features, follow the instructions on the **Prac4-8** tab of the practice file **MyPractice 4.xls**.

Hot Tip

The Page Break Preview command, found on the View menu, allows you to adjust what portion of the worksheet will fit onto one printed page. The data contained in the worksheet will be reduced to fit on the page if you expand the print range.

Shortcuts

Function	Button/Mouse	Menu	Keyboard
Drawing toolbar		Click View, then highlight Toolbars, then click Drawing	
Chart Wizard		Click Insert, then click Chart	
Format chart area (or selected chart object)		Click Format, then click Selected Chart Area (or other object)	[Ctrl]+[1]
Change chart type		Click Chart, then click Chart Type	
Add/Remove chart legend		Click Chart, then click Chart Options	
Plot chart data series by row		Click Chart, then click Source Data	
Plot chart data series by column		Click Chart, then click Source Data	

Identify Key Features

Figure 4-22 Identify features of the Excel screen

① ② ③ ④ ⑤ ⑥ ⑦ ⑧ ⑨

Microsoft Excel - Profit1.xls

File Edit View Insert Format Tools Data Window Help

Arial   10   B I U $ % ,

	A	B	C	D	E	F	G	H
1								
2				Income and Expenditures for Kay's Hound Accessories				
3	File name: Profit1.xls							
4	Author: Kay Samoy			Date: 4/6/98				
5	Ranges:			Macros:		Assumptions: Sales Growth		
6					Up 33% from			
7					Quarter 1			
8			ter 2	Quarter 3	Quarter 4	Total for Year		
9	Income							
10	Sales		000.00	1,173,700.00	1,291,070.00	4,501,770.00		
11								
12	Expenses							
13	Rent		000.00	45,000.00	45,000.00	180,000.00		
14	Salaries	30,000.00	30,000.00	51,750.00	61,750.00	173,500.00		
15	Misc.	10,200.00	8,188.00	7,900.00	9,940.00	36,228.00		
16	Total Expenses	85,200.00	83,188.00	104,650.00	116,690.00	389,728.00		
17								
18	Profit	$ 884,800.00	$ 983,812.00	$1,069,050.00	$1,174,380.00			
19								
20	Avg. Exp.	97,432						
21								
22								

Kay Samoy:
Miscellaneous
Profit
Quarter 1
Quarter 2
Quarter 3
Quarter 4
Rent
Salaries
Sales
Total Expenses

Sheet1 Sheet2 Sheet3

Draw   AutoShapes

Cell A5 commented by Kay Samoy   NUM

Select the Best Answer

10. Allows you to add text to a worksheet without worrying about cell constraints
11. Reduces the size of a dialog box so that you can easily view the worksheet
12. Appears along with your chart when you complete the Chart Wizard
13. Allows you to format any chart element from a dialog box
14. Indicates that a chart will be printed as opposed to the entire worksheet

a. Collapse dialog button
b. Double-clicking
c. Text box
d. Chart toolbar
e. Selected Chart radio button

Quiz (continued)

Complete the Statement

15. The Arrow tool can be found on the:

   a. Standard toolbar

   b. Formatting toolbar

   c. Drawing toolbar

   d. Shapes toolbar

16. To navigate between comments, use the:

   a. Comment toolbar

   b. Reviewing toolbar

   c. Standard toolbar

   d. Vertical scroll bar

17. All of the following are standard chart types except:

   a. Pie

   b. Doughnut

   c. Line

   d. Volume

18. You can add a title to a chart by using the:

   a. Chart Options dialog box

   b. Source Data dialog box

   c. Format Chart Area dialog box

   d. Chart Type dialog box

19. To maintain a chart's center point when resizing it:

   a. Press [Ctrl] while dragging the chart

   b. Press [Shift] while dragging a sizing handle

   c. Press [Ctrl] while dragging a sizing handle

   d. Press [Tab] while dragging a sizing handle

20. You can change all of the following chart aspects from the 3-D View dialog box with the exception of:

   a. Elevation

   b. Rotation

   c. Height

   d. Location

Interactivity

Test Your Skills

1. Add objects and graphics to a spreadsheet:

   a. Open the file **Test 3.xls** that you created at the end of Lesson 3.

   b. Add a text box that says **Best day for relaxation and errands** above the day of the week column of your choice.

   c. Use the Fill Color palette to add color to the text box.

   d. Draw an arrow from the text box to the appropriate day of the week label.

   e. Use the Line Color palette to add color to the arrow.

   f. Enter a comment that displays the names of all your defined ranges in the cell that contains the Ranges label.

2. Create a chart based on your worksheet data:

   a. Select the Average range in your worksheet by using the Name box.

   b. Use the Chart Wizard to create a basic pie chart that plots each daily activity as a percentage of the total time you spend on all of your activities during an average day.

   c. In Step 2 of the Wizard, use the Series tab to select the appropriate Category Labels for your chart.

   d. In Step 3, choose a title for the chart, leave the legend displayed on the right, and show percent data labels.

   e. In Step 4, insert the chart into the current worksheet.

3. Move, resize, and format a chart:

   a. Move the chart so that it is centered below the data portion of the worksheet.

   b. Adjust the borders of the chart and the legend so that no chart elements obscure each other. Make any other size and placement adjustments that you think will improve the appearance of the chart.

   c. Change the chart's sub-type to a **3-D Exploded pie**.

   d. Increase the elevation of the pie by thirty degrees, and rotate it twenty degrees counter-clockwise.

   e. Change the color of the largest pie slice in the chart.

   f. Add a shadow to your chart's title and fill the title box with color.

4. Save and print the changes you have made to the spreadsheet:

   a. Save the file as **Test 4.xls**.

   b. Preview the worksheet and use the Page Setup dialog box to make it fit on one page if necessary.

   c. Print a copy of the entire worksheet.

   d. Print a copy of just the chart.

Interactivity (continued)

Problem Solving

A friend of yours is considering learning Microsoft Excel. You want to convince your friend that the task is well worthwhile. In order to do this, you plan to show him or her the spreadsheets you have created while learning Excel. First, however, you decide to incorporate the latest techniques you have learned into the spreadsheets so that they are truly impressive. Return to the files **Solved 2.xls** and **Solved 3.xls**, and add at least one text box, one comment, and a chart to each. Use these features to call attention to and further illustrate important data in the worksheets. Be sure to save the additions you make to the files.

LESSON

USING MACROS

When working with a spreadsheet, you may find that you use certain commands and perform certain tasks over and over again. You can automate these tasks by creating a macro. A macro is a set of instructions that executes commands in a specified order. For example, you can create a macro that removes the gridlines from the active worksheet. Removing the gridlines from a worksheet is a multistep process; a macro reduces the operation to a single step.

Careful planning is essential in the creation of a macro. It is a good idea to outline the commands your macro will perform so you can achieve the desired results.

A macro is created by recording a series of commands and keystrokes as they would normally be performed in the course of completing the necessary actions. As you record a macro, each action is translated into programming code that you can later view and modify. Once a macro is recorded it can be played back at any time to perform the recorded commands in one step. If the macro does not work exactly as you planned, it can be edited so as to remove or add functionality. A macro can be added to a toolbar as a button or to a menu as a command.

Case Study:
Kay will be creating a macro to calculate estimated sales growth in different increments to see how it will affect the rest of her worksheet.

Recording a Macro

Concept

Once you have figured out what steps you would like your macro to perform, you are ready to begin recording it.

Do It!

Kay will record a macro that prints out five copies of her worksheet, each with a different value for projected sales growth.

1 Open the file named **DoIt 5-1** from your student folder and save it as **Profit2.xls**.

2 Click **Tools**, then click **Record New Macro** on the Macro submenu. The Record Macro dialog box appears, as shown in Figure 5-1.

3 Type **Sales_Projection** to name the macro. Be sure to include the underscore ([Shift]+[-]), since macro names cannot contain any spaces.

4 Click the Shortcut key text box, then type **[m]**. This determines that the macro you are about to record will run when [Ctrl]+[m] is pressed.

5 Click to the right of **Samoy** in the the Description text box, then press **[Enter]** to begin a new line.

6 Type **changes sales growth figure and prints the page** to add it to the macro's description.

7 Click [OK]. The Record Macro dialog box will close, the Stop Recording toolbar opens (if it does not, select Stop Recording from the Toolbars submenu on the View menu), and the status bar will read Ready Recording, indicating that you can begin recording your macro.

8 Click cell **H5** to select it.

9 Type **5** to change the Sales Growth assumption, click the **Enter** button ✓ to confirm the new entry (notice that the data in the worksheet is recalculated to reflect this change), then click the **Print** button 🖨 to send a copy of the newly calculated data to the printer.

10 Repeat the above step four times, substituting **10**, **15**, **20**, and **25** for the Sales Growth assumption respectively each time.

11 Click the **Stop Recording** button ■ (see Figure 5-2). The Stop Recording toolbar will close. Your macro has been recorded.

12 Save your workbook.

More

By default, the macro recorder uses absolute cell references when it records. If you would like to use relative cell references in your macro, click the **Relative Reference** button 🗗 on the Stop Recording toolbar before you select a cell. The button will remain depressed, indicating that relative cell references are being recorded, until it is clicked again, to revert to absolute cell references.

Figure 5-1 Record Macro dialog box

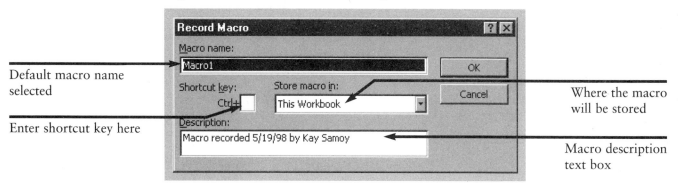

Default macro name
selected

Enter shortcut key here

Where the macro
will be stored

Macro description
text box

Figure 5-2 Recording a macro

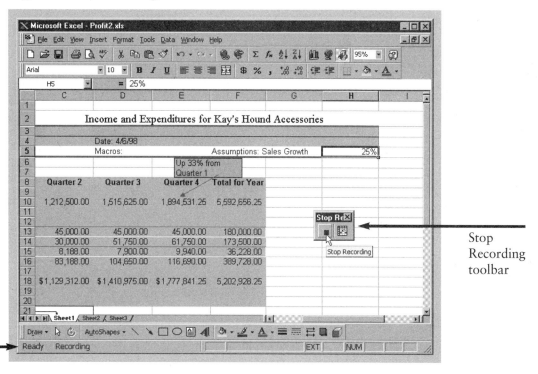

Stop
Recording
toolbar

Status bar indicating
that recording is in
progress

Practice

To practice recording a macro, open the
practice file **Practice-Lesson 5.xls**, save it
as **MyPractice5**, and then follow the
instructions on the **Prac5-1** sheet.

Hot Tip

You can take as much time as necessary to
record a macro, without having to worry
about pauses between actions. Excel will
play back the series of commands in suc-
cession without any pauses.

Running a Macro

Concept

Once you have recorded a macro, it can be run at any time within the workbook it was created. It is a good idea to test a macro you have recorded to ensure that it works as intended.

Do It!

Kay wants to run the macro she recorded in order to make sure that it was recorded correctly.

1 Click **Tools**, then select **Macros** from the Macro submenu. The Macro dialog box opens with the macro Sales_Projection selected in the macros list field and appearing in the Macro name text box, as shown in Figure 5-3.

2 Click [Run]. The Macro dialog box will close and the macro will be executed. If your macro ran correctly, five pages should have been sent to the printer with the data in cell H5 displaying 5 to 25% in five percent increments.

3 Click cell **D5** to select it.

4 Click once in the formula bar, to the right of **Macros:**. A flashing insertion point will appear.

5 Type [Space], [Space], **Sales_Projection** to document your macro, then press [**Enter**]. Your worksheet should now appear like the one shown in Figure 5-4.

6 Save your workbook.

More

The Macro dialog box offers several buttons that allow you to manipulate your macro. In the above exercise, you used the Run button to initiate your macro. The Cancel button closes the Macro dialog box and returns you to the active worksheet. The Step Into and Edit buttons open the Microsoft Visual Basic application, which can be used to work with the actual code or programming language of the macro. Clicking the **Step Into** button opens Visual Basic in debugging mode, allowing you to run the macro while pausing at predetermined points so you can ascertain where possible errors may be occurring. The Delete button erases the selected macro. The Options button opens the Macro Options dialog box, which lets you edit the macro's description and alter the shortcut key that runs the macro.

Figure 5-3 Macro dialog box

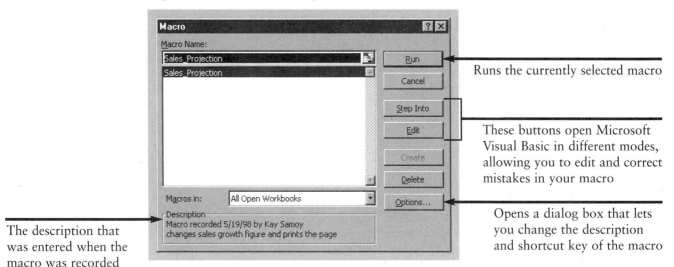

Runs the currently selected macro

These buttons open Microsoft Visual Basic in different modes, allowing you to edit and correct mistakes in your macro

Opens a dialog box that lets you change the description and shortcut key of the macro

The description that was entered when the macro was recorded

Figure 5-4 Documenting a macro

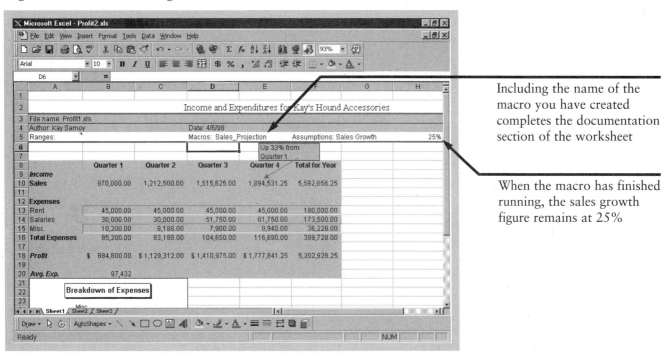

Including the name of the macro you have created completes the documentation section of the worksheet

When the macro has finished running, the sales growth figure remains at 25%

Practice

To practice running a macro follow the instructions on the **Prac5-2** tab of the practice file **MyPractice5.xls**.

Hot Tip

To stop a macro before it has finished running, press **[Esc]**.

Editing a Macro

Concept

If you would like to alter the function of a macro, you do not necessarily have to rerecord it. When a macro is first recorded, Excel keeps a record of each command and action that you undertake in programming code, which you can then view and manipulate using Microsoft Visual Basic. Though unwieldy for making major changes, the Edit Macro function can be very helpful when only small modifications are necessary.

Do It!

Kay wants to edit the macro she has created so that it will return the worksheet to its original state when the macro is finished running.

1 Click **Tools**, then click **Macro** on the **Macros** submenu. The Macro dialog box will open.

2 Click [Edit] to open Visual Basic. The Visual Basic window and its components are shown in Figure 5-5. Look over the steps of your macro, which should match those in the Profit2.xls - Module1(Code) window. Each line corresponds with an action that was taken when the macro was recorded.

3 Select the fifth line in the main body of the macro, as shown in Figure 5-5. This line of code instructs Excel to change the contents of the active cell to 10%.

4 Click **Edit**, then click **Copy** to send a copy of this line of code to the Clipboard.

5 Click once after the last line in the main body of the macro code, then press [Enter]. The insertion point should now be located in a blank line above the End Sub heading.

6 Click **Edit**, then click **Paste** to insert the copied line of code into the macro at the insertion point. With this new line of code inserted, the original value of 10% will be restored as the sales growth assumption when the macro has finished running. Your macro code should now match that shown in Figure 5-6.

7 Click the **Close** button [X] at the upper right of the Microsoft Visual Basic window to close it and return to the worksheet.

8 Save your worksheet to incorporate the changes you have made to the macro.

More

You can add **comments** to the code in your macro so that you or others will be able to easily understand the function of a particular line or section of the macro's code. Entering an apostrophe (') before a line of text marks it as a comment, and it will appear green to indicate its status. Notice the comment section above the macro code in Figure 5-6; each line that begins with an apostrophe is displayed in green and will be ignored by Excel when executing the macro.

Figure 5-5 Editing a macro with Microsoft Visual Basic

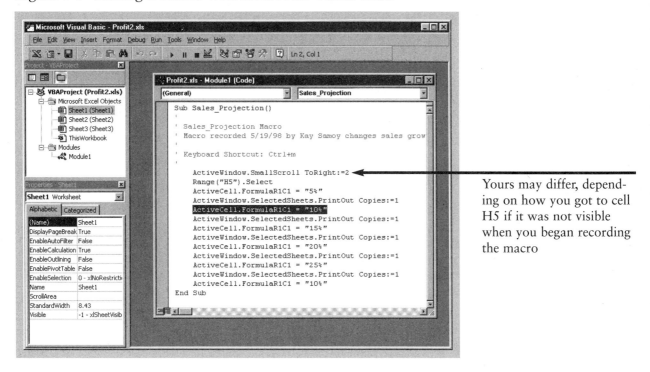

Yours may differ, depending on how you got to cell H5 if it was not visible when you began recording the macro

Figure 5-6 Edited macro

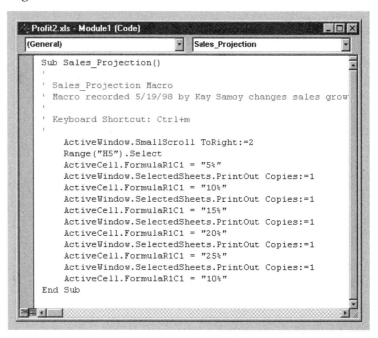

Practice

To practice editing a macro follow the instructions on the **Prac5-3** tab of the practice file **MyPractice5.xls**.

Hot Tip

Pressing **[Alt]+[F11]** when in Excel will open the Visual Basic Editor.

Adding a Macro to a Toolbar

Concept

A macro can be placed on a menu so that it can be accessed more easily, or can be displayed as a button on a toolbar.

Do It!

Kay has decided that she wants to put a button on one of her toolbars that would activate the macro she has made.

1 Click **Tools**, then click **Customize**. The Customize dialog box appears.

2 Click the **Commands** tab to bring it to the front if it is not already there. The Categories area of this tab contains a list of menus, toolbars, and other locations where commands can be stored. The Commands section lists the commands that pertain to the selected category.

3 Scroll to the bottom of the Categories section and click **Macros** to select it. It will appear highlighted, as shown in Figure 5-7, to indicate its selection, and two custom commands appear in the Commands section.

4 Click the **Custom Button** icon and drag it out of the dialog box and the the right end of the Standard toolbar. The mouse pointer will change to ⬚ as it is dragged over the document widow. The x in the box indicates that the button cannot be dropped there, but the pointer will change to ⬚ when it is over a toolbar or menu. A short vertical line will appear on the toolbar indicating where the dropped button will be inserted; place the button at the far right of the toolbar, after the Office Assistant button. The button appears where you inserted it, with a black border surrounding it to notify you that it is selected for modification, as shown in Figure 5-8.

5 Click [Modify Selection ▾] , then click **Assign Macro** on the menu that appears. The Assign Macro dialog box opens, with name of the macro you have made displayed.

6 Click the name of the macro, **Sales_Projection**, to make it appear in the Macro Name box; then click [OK] . The button will now activate the selected macro when clicked.

Figure 5-7 Customize dialog box

Contains a list of all Excel toolbars; check items to make them
appear on the Commands tab
for customization

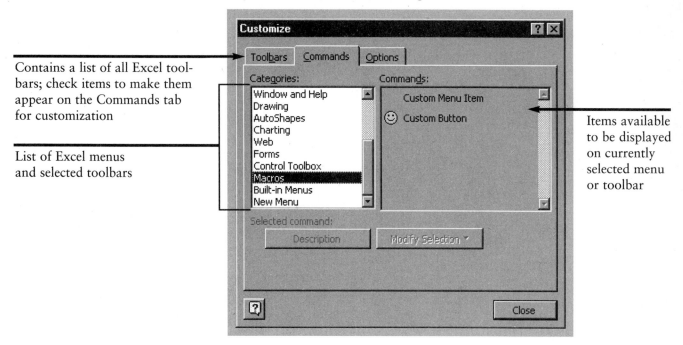

Items available
to be displayed
on currently
selected menu
or toolbar

List of Excel menus
and selected toolbars

Figure 5-8 Inserting a button into a toolbar

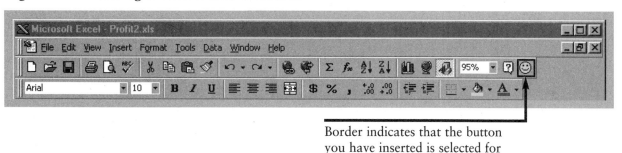

Border indicates that the button
you have inserted is selected for
modification

Adding a Macro
to a Toolbar (continued)

Do It!

7 Click [Modify Selection ▾] , then triple-click the **Name** text box near the top of the menu to select its contents.

8 Type **Sales_Projection** to name the button you have inserted; this will appear as the button's ScreenTip when you have finished.

9 Click **Change Button Image** on the Modify Selection menu, then click the **calculator** button 🖩 on the palette of possible buttons that appears, shown in Figure 5-9. The image on the button you inserted changes from a smiley face to a calculator.

10 Click [Close] . The dialog box closes, and the black border around the button disappears. The button is now active, and will run the designated macro if clicked. The toolbar on your screen should resemble the one in Figure 5-10.

11 Click the Sales_projection button [Close] run your macro. Notice that the value in cell H5 is returned to 10% at the completion of the macro, reflecting the change you made in the previous skill.

12 Save your workbook.

More

You can drag a command from the Customize dialog box onto a menu instead of a toolbar. When the pointer is over a menu the menu will open, and a horizontal line that follows the mouse pointer will show where on the menu the selected command will appear when inserted, just as a small vertical line indicated where the command would be placed on a toolbar as a button.

When the Customize dialog box is open, buttons and menus can be selected and modified. Right-clicking a button or a command on a menu will bring up the Modify Command menu. The two Text Only commands let you control how a command appears. Selecting the **Text Only (Always)** command while the macro button is selected would make the button appear as [Sales_Projection] on a toolbar or menu. The **Text Only (in Menus)** command will make a menu command appear as text, without its assigned button icon next to it. The **Image and Text** command makes commands appear with both their names and their button icons whether they are located on a menu or a toolbar.

Though Excel provides many icons to use on buttons that you create, you can also design your own. Click Edit Button Image on the Modify Command menu to bring up the **Button Editor** dialog box, shown in Figure 5-11. To change the color of one of the small squares (representing a single pixel) in the icon, just click it. The pixel will change to match the currently selected color. The Move section allows you to nudge the contents of the picture up, down, left or right, without having to redraw the entire image.

Figure 5-9 A palette of buttons from which
to choose on the Modify Command menu

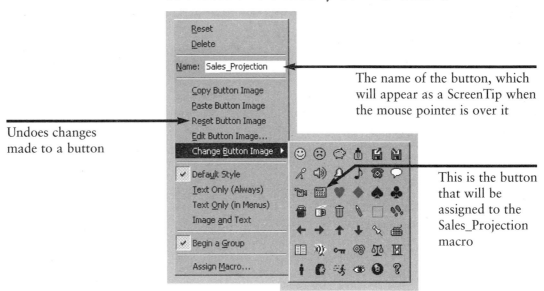

Undoes changes
made to a button

The name of the button, which
will appear as a ScreenTip when
the mouse pointer is over it

This is the button
that will be
assigned to the
Sales_Projection
macro

Figure 5-10 Modified macro button

Proper appearance of the
macro button and its
ScreenTip

Figure 5-11 Button Editor dialog box

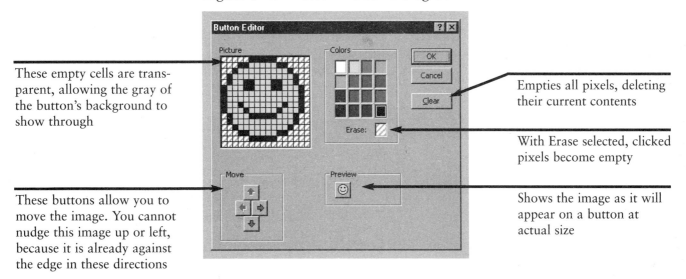

These empty cells are trans-
parent, allowing the gray of
the button's background to
show through

Empties all pixels, deleting
their current contents

With Erase selected, clicked
pixels become empty

These buttons allow you to
move the image. You cannot
nudge this image up or left,
because it is already against
the edge in these directions

Shows the image as it will
appear on a button at
actual size

Practice

To practice adding a macro to a toolbar,
follow the instructions on the **Prac5-4** tab
of the practice file **MyPractice5.xls**.

Hot Tip

To remove a toolbar button or menu command, open the Customize dialog box and
drag the desired item from its toolbar or
menu to the dialog box.

Copying Macros Across Files

Concept

A macro that is created in a workbook can be used by any other open workbook if the macro's parent workbook is open. If there is a shortcut for a macro, such as a toolbar button or menu command, and the parent file for the macro is not open, initiating the shortcut will cause Excel to open the macro's parent workbook before it applies the macro in the active workbook. **Copying** a macro from one workbook to another increases efficiency by allowing you to run the macro without having to first open its parent file.

Do It!

Kay wants to copy her macro, Sales_Projection, from Profit2.xls to a workbook that contains her future business income and expenditures so that she can use it there.

1. Open **Doit 5-5.xls** from your student disk. The workbook will be displayed in the window as the active document with Profit2 open behind it. This workbook is similar to Profit2.xls, but is for the following year's sales and expenses, and lacks a chart or a macro.

2. Save Doit 5-5.xls as **Profit99.xls** in your student files. The workbook should now appear like the one shown in Figure 5-12.

3. Click **Tools**, highlight **Macro**, then select **Visual Basic Editor** from the submenu. Figure 5-13 displays the Microsoft Visual Basic window that will open.

4. The Project window in the Visual Basic window displays the hierarchy of each of the open workbooks as icons labeled VBAProject (Profit2.xls) and VBA Project (Profit99.xls), with their contents nested below. Click the ⊞ next to the upper icon. This will expand the hierarchy so you can view all the folders associated with that particular file. The Microsoft Excel Objects folder contains the worksheets for the workbook.

5. Click the ⊞ next to the Modules folder of Profit2.xls. The contents of the folder, Module1, will be displayed, as shown in Figure 5-14. The Modules folder houses the macros for the workbook, and Module1 is the macro you created. Notice that the representation of Profit99.xls does not show a Modules folder since this file does not contain a macro.

Figure 5-12 Kay's worksheet for the following year

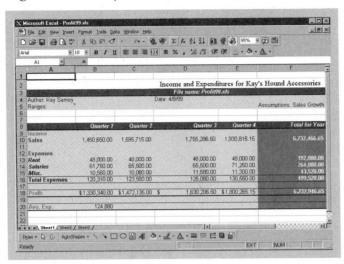

Figure 5-13 Visual Basic Editor

Click to show the folder's contents

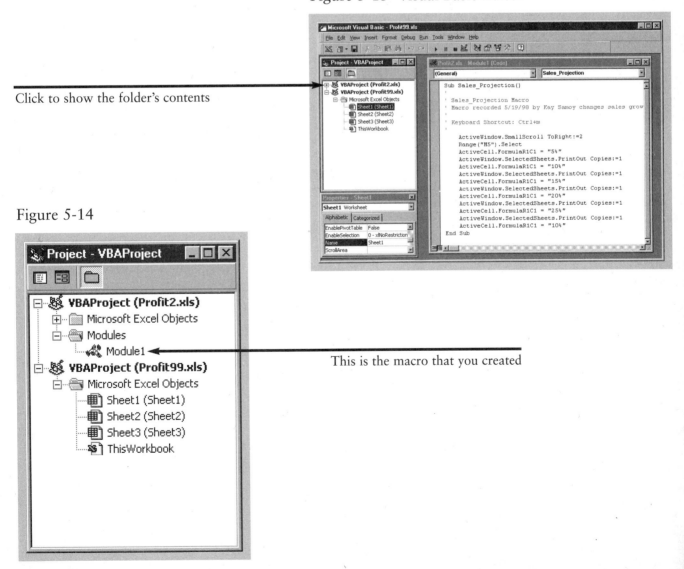

Figure 5-14

This is the macro that you created

Copying Macros
Across Files (continued)

Do It!

6 Click and drag **Module1** onto the **VBAProject (Profit99.xls)** icon, releasing the mouse button when VBAProject (Profit99.xls) becomes highlighted (Figure 5-15). A new folder called Modules will appear in the VBAProject (Profit99.xls) hierarchy, shown in Figure 5-16, containing the copied macro.

7 Click the **Close** button on the Visual Basic title bar to close the window.

8 Click **Window**, then click **Profit2.xls** to make it the active document window.

9 Close the file by clicking its **Close** button on the menu bar. The workbook will close, leaving Profit99.xls as the only open workbook.

10 Press [Ctrl]+[m] to run the macro. The macro will run as it did with Profit2.xls.

11 Close **Profit99.xls**, saving changes when prompted to do so.

More

When you recorded the Sales_Projection macro it was saved only within the open workbook, Profit2.xls. This occurred because the default setting, This Workbook, was left unchanged in the Store macro in section of the Record Macro dialog box when you created the macro. In the above skill, you copied a macro to make it available to a workbook other than the macro's parent file. Copying is a good way to share case-specific macros, such as the Sales_Projection macro, between workbooks. However, if you create a macro that will be useful in many types of workbooks, such as one that inserts a custom header, copying it from workbook to workbook every time you want to use it would be tedious.

The **Personal Macro Workbook** lets you store macros so that they will be available to all Excel workbooks. You can save a macro directly into the Personal Macro Workbook by selecting Personal Macro Workbook in the Store macro in section of the Record Macro dialog box when you record the macro. This creates a workbook called Personal.xls in the Xlstart folder. A previously recorded macro can be copied to the Personal Macro Workbook in the same way that you copied macros between workbooks above. Once created, the Personal Macro Workbook will appear in the Visual Basic Project - VBAProject window just as any other workbook, and can be manipulated in the same manner. This workbook will be opened by Excel so as to make all of the macros it contains available to all open workbooks. Personal.xls is hidden by Excel so that it does not interfere with your work.

Figure 5-15 Copying a macro to another workbook

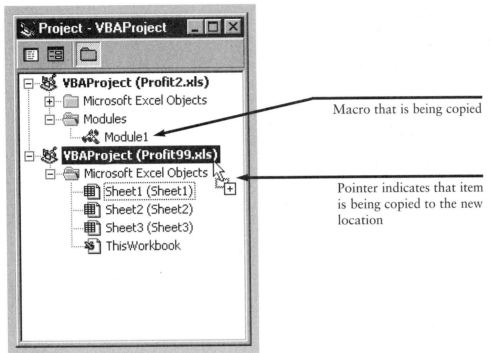

Macro that is being copied

Pointer indicates that item
is being copied to the new
location

Figure 5-16 File hierarchy with copied macro

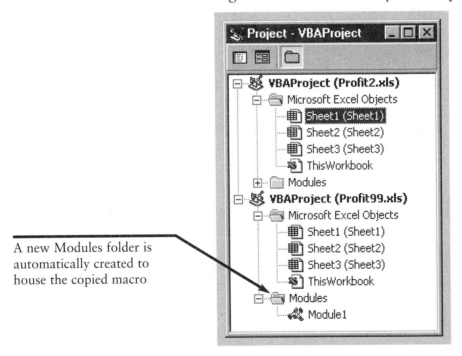

A new Modules folder is
automatically created to
house the copied macro

Practice

To practice copying a macro across workbooks, create a new workbook, save it as
MyPractice5-5.xls, then copy the
Expense_Report_Header macro to the new
workbook. Save both workbooks when
you are finished.

Hot Tip

When you create a toolbar button or menu
command for a macro, the shortcut
becomes linked to the parent workbook of
the macro. Therefore, if you use the toolbar
button for the Sales_Projection macro,
Profit2.xls will open if it is not already.

Shortcuts

Function	Menu	Keyboard
Open Macro dialog box	Click Tools, highlight Macro, then click Macros	[Alt]+[F8]
Open Visual Basic Editor	Click Tools, highlight Macro, then click Visual Basic Editor	[Alt]+[F11]
Run a macro	Click Tools, highlight Macro, click Macros, then select a macro and click Run	[Ctrl]+[Assigned short-cut key]
Interrupt a running macro		[Esc]

Identify Key Features

Figure 5-17 Identify components and concepts of macro editing

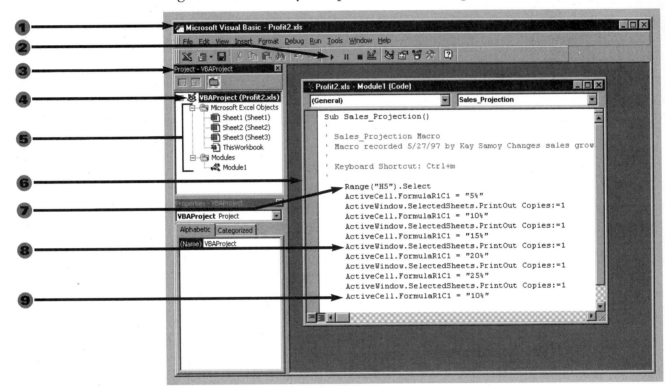

Select the Best Answer

10. A set of instructions that automates tasks you perform often

11. Contains general commands for working with macros

12. Allows you to make changes to a macro you have already recorded

13. Opens Visual Basic in a debugging mode

14. Click this to change the default way of referencing cells in a macro

a. Step Into button

b. Macro

c. Relative Reference button

d. Tools menu

e. Visual Basic Editor

Quiz (continued)

Complete the Statement

15. Using the Macro Options dialog box, you can edit:

    a. A macro's name

    b. A macro's name and description

    c. A macro's description and shortcut key

    d. A macro's name and shortcut key

16. To make a macro available to all workbooks, store it in the:

    a. My Documents folder

    b. Current workbook

    c. All-Macro Workbook

    d. Personal Macro Workbook

17. You can determine all of the following in the Record Macro dialog box except the:

    a. Macro's name

    b. Macro's steps

    c. Place the macro will be stored

    d. Macro's shortcut key

18. The Relative Reference button is located on the:

    a. Stop Recording toolbar

    b. Macro toolbar

    c. Record toolbar

    d. Visual Basic toolbar

19. To add a macro to a toolbar, access the Customize dialog box from the:

    a. Macro dialog box

    b. Options dialog box

    c. Tools menu

    d. Options menu

20. If you use a shortcut to a macro that has not been copied to the current workbook, Excel will:

    a. Run the macro

    b. Create a parent workbook for the macro

    c. Delete the shortcut

    d. Open the macro's parent workbook

Interactivity

Test Your Skills

1. Record a macro that will calculate the average time you spend doing an activity over the five days of the work week.

   a. Open the file **Test 4.xls**, which you created at the end of Lesson 4.

   b. Place a label that reads **5 Day Average** directly to the right of the Average label.

   c. Select the cell where the 5 Day Average column intersects with the Class row.

   d. Open the Record Macro dialog box. Name the macro **Five_Day_Average**, make the shortcut key **[Ctrl]+[m]**, and add a second line to the description that reads **Calculates average for Monday thru Friday**.

   e. When you click OK in the Macro dialog box, the Stop Recording toolbar should appear. If not, activate it from the View menu.

   f. Begin recording the macro: click the Relative Reference button; click the **Paste Function** button; select the Average function; when the Average dialog box asks for **Number 1**, collapse the dialog box; select the cells that contain the Class data for Monday through Friday; expand the dialog box and click OK; click the Stop Recording button.

   g. When you stopped recording the macro, the average time you spend in class Monday through Friday should have appeared in the Class row of the 5 Day Average column.

2. Run the macro:

   a. Select the cell in the Activities row of the 5 Day Average column.

   b Open the Macro dialog box.

   c. Run the Five_Day_Average macro to calculate the time you spend participating in activities Monday through Friday.

   d. Select the cell in the Meals row of the 5 Day Average column.

   e. Run the Five_Day_Average macro using its shortcut key.

   f. Use the macro you created to calculate the five day averages for the remaining daily activities.

3. View the code for the macro you created:

   a. Open the Visual Basic Editor.

   b. Select Module 1 in the Project window, and look over its code (if the code is not visible, click the View Code button).

   c. Close Microsoft Visual Basic.

4. Add a button for the Five_Day_Average macro to the Standard toolbar and save the workbook as **Test 5.xls**.

Interactivity (continued)

Problem Solving

Oliver's bakery is a newly opened take-out store in your town that features a variety of bagels, fresh breads, croissants, cookies, and coffee. Demand for freshly prepared take-out food is high, so business is booming. The owner of Oliver's, Oliver Rhodes, has already had to hire six employees. Oliver currently processes the payroll manually. He makes all of the calculations for salary, deductions, and net pay using a hand-held calculator. Then he types the results onto a payroll register sheet. A payroll register is a report prepared for each payroll period that lists the names, gross pay, deductions, and net pay for each employee, and the total gross pay, deductions, and net pay for that payroll period.

Oliver would like to use his time more effectively to promote his business and to develop new varieties of baked goods and coffee. He also wants to curb the danger of making miscalculations in the payroll. Oliver feels that since there are relatively few checks to write, this part of the process can remain manual. However, he could save many hours if all of the payroll calculations and the preparation of the Payroll Register report could be automated.

It is your job to develop a worksheet that creates a payroll register report for Oliver's. The basic format of the payroll register includes the pay period and the employee's names, social security numbers, hours worked, and hourly pay rate. The worksheet should automatically calculate weekly gross pay, net pay, and all deductions for each employee. It should also provide totals for each of these categories for the pay period. Weekly gross pay can be calculated by multiplying pay rate by hours worked. Net pay is gross pay minus all deductions. Use the following figures to calculated deductions: Federal withholding tax = 9.25 % of gross pay; State withholding tax = 2.5% of gross pay; Social Security (FICA) = 6.2% of gross pay; Medicare = 1.45% of gross pay. Enter these figures as assumptions in your worksheet.

It is up to you to create the hours worked and pay rate data, so use realistic figures. When constructing the worksheet, be sure to take advantage of Excel's most useful features such as formatting, cell referencing, formulas, and macros. The payroll register report should fit on one page when you print it. When you have finished, save the file to your student disk as **Solved 5.xls**.

Glossary

A

Absolute cell reference
A cell reference that will remain fixed, even if the formula containing the reference is moved. To make a cell reference absolute, place a dollar sign ($), before both the column letter and row number.

Active cell
The currently selected cell on a worksheet, indicated by the cell pointer.

Alignment
The horizontal position of values or labels within a cell (for example, left, right, or center).

Anchor cells
The first and last cells in a cell range; the cells used to express a range address (for example, B9:E9).

Animated border
Indicates that a cell's contents have been sent to the Clipboard.

Argument
Information such as a cell address, range, or value, enclosed in parentheses, used by a function or macro to produce a result.

Arithmetic operators
Symbols used by Excel to perform formula calculations such as +,-,*, and /.

Assumption
A variable factor that is useful for conducting what-if analysis in a worksheet.

AutoCalculate box
Automatically displays the total of the values in a selected group of cells in the status bar.

AutoComplete
Automatically finishes entering a label when its first letter(s) match that of a label used previously in the column.

AutoFill
Automatically fills a range with series information such as the days of the week when the range after the first value is selected using the fill handle.

AutoFormat
Adds a predesigned set of formatting to selected ranges. AutoFormats can modify numbers, borders, fonts, patterns, alignment, and height and width of rows and columns.

AutoSum
A function that automatically adds the values in the cells directly above or to the left of the active cell.

C

Cancel button
Removes the contents of a cell and restores the cell's previous contents if there were any; marked by an X on the formula bar.

Cell
The space formed by the intersection of a row and a column; the basic unit of a worksheet.

Cell address
A cell's identification code, composed of the letter and number of the column and row that intersect to form the cell (for example, B22).

Cell pointer
The black rectangle that outlines the active cell.

Cell reference
A cell address used to refer to a cell in a formula. Cell references can be relative or absolute.

Chart
A graphic representation of values and their relationships, used to identify trends and contrasts in data.

Chart Wizard
A series of specialized dialog boxes that guide you through the creation or modification of a chart.

Check box
A small square box that allows you to turn a dialog box option on or off by clicking it.

Clipboard

A temporary storage area for cut or copied text or graphics. You can paste the contents of the Clipboard into any cell, worksheet, or even another application file. The Clipboard holds information until it replaced by another piece of data, or until the computer is shut down.

Close

To quit an application and remove its window from the screen. You can also close a file while leaving the application open. The Close button appears in the upper right corner of the application or worksheet window.

Column selector button

The gray rectangle that appears above each column and displays its column letter.

Comment

An electronic note that can be attached to a cell. Similar to a text box, but can be hidden from view.

Contents and Index

A comprehensive help facility that organizes information by category and alphabetically, and also lets you search for help topics using key words.

Control menu

Contains commands relating to resizing, moving, and closing a window.

Copy

To place a duplicate of a file, or portion thereof, on the Clipboard to be pasted in another location.

Cut

To remove a file, or a portion of a file, and place it on the Clipboard.

D

Data series

The selected data taken from a worksheet and converted into a chart.

Delete

To remove the contents from a cell or an object such as a chart from the worksheet.

Dialog box

A box that offers additional command options for you to review or change before executing the command.

Documentation

The first section of a worksheet. It contains important information such as the spreadsheet's author, purpose, date of creation, file name, macros, and ranges.

Drawing toolbar

Contains tools for creating and formatting shapes, text boxes, and WordArt.

Dummy row/column

A blank row or column at the end of a defined range that holds a place so that Excel can recalculate formulas correctly if a new row or column is added to the range.

E

Edit

To add, delete, or modify cell contents or other elements of a file.

Electronic spreadsheet application

A computer program designed to organize information in columns and rows on a worksheet and facilitate performing rapid and accurate calculations on groups of interrelated numbers.

Ellipsis

Three dots (...) after a command that indicate a dialog box will follow with options for executing the command.

Enter button

Confirms cell entries. The Enter button is located on the formula bar and is symbolized by a check mark.

Exploded pie slice

A pie chart slice that has been dragged away from the rest of the pie to emphasize it.

F

Fill handle

The small black square at the bottom right corner of the cell pointer. Dragging the fill handle copies a cell's contents to adjacent cells or fills a range with series information.

Floating toolbar

A toolbar housed in its own window rather than along an edge of a window. All toolbars in Excel 97 can be dragged to a floating position.

Folders

Subdivisions of a disk that function as a filing system to help you organize files.

Font

A name given to a collection of text characters of a certain size, weight, and style. Font has become synonymous with typeface. Arial and Times New Roman are examples of font names.

Format
The way information appears on a page. To format means to change the appearance of data without changing its content.

Formula
A combination of cell addresses and operators that instructs Excel to perform calculations such as adding, subtracting, multiplying, or averaging.

Formula bar
The area below the Formatting toolbar that displays cell contents, whether they are labels, values, or formulas. You may enter and edit cell contents in the formula bar rather than in the cell itself.

Function
A built-in formula included in Excel that makes it easy for you to perform common calculations.

G

Go To
A useful command for moving great distances across a worksheet.

Gridlines
Vertical and horizontal lines on a chart that delineate the cells' boundaries.

I

Input
The data you enter into a worksheet and work with to produce results.

Insertion point
A vertical blinking line on the screen that indicates where text and graphics will be inserted. The insertion point also indicates where an action will begin.

L

Label
Text or numbers that describe the data you place in rows and columns. Labels should be entered in a worksheet first to define the rows and columns and are automatically left-aligned by Excel.

Label prefix
A typed character that marks an entry as a label. For example, if you type an apostrophe before a number, it will be treated as label rather than as a value.

Landscape
A term used to refer to horizontal page orientation; opposite of "portrait," or vertical, orientation.

Launch
To start a program so you can work with it.

Legend
The section of a chart that details which colors or patterns on a chart represent which information.

M

Macro
A set of instructions that automates a specific multi-step task that you perform frequently, reducing the process to one command.

Menu
A list of related application commands.

Menu bar
Lists the names of menus containing application commands. Click a menu name on the menu bar to display its list of commands.

Merge and Center
Combines two or more adjacent cells into a single cell and places the contents of the upper left-most cell at the center of the new cell.

Mouse pointer
The usually arrow-shaped cursor on the screen that you control by guiding the mouse on your desk. You use the mouse pointer to select items, drag objects, choose commands, and start or exit programs. The shape of the mouse pointer can change depending on the task being executed.

N

Name box
The box at the left end of the formula bar that displays the address of the active cell or the name of a selected range that has been defined and named. You can also use the drop-down arrow in the Name box to select a named range.

O

Object
An item such as a chart or graphic that that can be relocated and resized independently of the structure of the worksheet.

Office Assistant
An animated representation of the Microsoft Office 97 help facility. The Office Assistant provides hints, instructions, and a convenient interface between the user and Excel's various help features.

Open
Command used to access a file that has already been created and saved on disk.

Order of operations
The order Excel follows when calculating formulas with multiple operations: (1) exponents, (2) multiplication and division from left to right, (3) addition and subtraction from left to right. In addition, operations inside parenthesis are calculated first, using the above order.

Output
The results produced by calculations done on the input data of a worksheet.

P

Paste
To insert cut or copied data held in the Clipboard into other cells, worksheets, or workbooks.

Paste Function
Command that allows you to choose and perform a calculation without entering its formula on the keyboard.

Paste Special
Allows you to paste the contents of a cell using formatting characteristics that you specify.

Personal Macro Workbook
Allows you to store macros so that they will be available to all Excel workbooks.

Point size
A measurement used for the size of text characters and row height. There are 72 points in 1 inch.

Portrait
A term used to refer to vertical page orientation; opposite of "landscape," or horizontal, orientation.

Print Preview
Allows you to view your worksheet as it will appear when printed on a sheet of paper.

Program
A software application such as Microsoft Word or Microsoft Excel that performs specific tasks.

Programs menu
A menu on the Windows 95 Start menu that lists the applications on your computer such as Microsoft Excel.

R

Radio button
A small circular button in a dialog box that allows you to turn options on or off.

RAM (random access memory)
The memory that programs use to function while the computer is on. When you shut down the computer, all information in RAM is lost.

Range
A group of two or more cells, usually adjacent.

Range name
A name chosen for a selected group of cells that describes the data they contain.

Record New Macro
Command used to name and perform the series of actions that Excel will store as a macro.

Relative cell reference
Allows a formula to be moved to a new location on a worksheet. The formula will then follow the same directional instructions from the new starting point using new cell references.

Relative Reference button
Instructs Excel to treat cells used while recording a macro as relative references.

Reviewing toolbar
Contains commands for inserting, deleting, displaying, and navigating between comments.

Right-click
To click the right mouse button; often used to access specialized menus and shortcuts.

Row height
The measurement of a cell from top to bottom.

Row selector button
The gray rectangle that appears to the left of each row and displays its row number.

Run
To start an application. Also refers to initiating the steps of a macro.

S

Save
Stores changes you have made to a file, maintaining the file's current name and location.

Save As
Command used to save a new file, for the first time or to create a duplicate copy of a file that has already been saved.

ScreenTip

A brief explanation of a button or object that appears when the mouse pointer is passed over it. Other ScreenTips are accessed by using the What's This? feature on the Help menu or by clicking the question mark button in a dialog box.

Scroll bar

A graphical device for moving vertically and horizontally through a document with the mouse. Scroll bars are located along the right and bottom edges of the document window.

Scroll bar box

A small gray box located inside a scroll bar that indicates your current position relative to the rest of the document window. You can advance a scroll bar box by dragging it, clicking the scroll bar on either side of it, or by clicking the scroll arrows.

Select All button

The gray rectangle in the upper left corner of the worksheet where the row and column headings meet. Clicking the Select All button highlights the entire worksheet.

Series of labels

A range of incremental labels created by entering the first label in the series and then dragging the fill handle the number of cells desired. Excel automatically enters the remaining labels in order.

Sheet

The term Excel uses to refer to an individual worksheet (Sheet 1, Sheet 2, etc.).

Sheet tab scrolling buttons

Allow you to access sheet tabs that are not visible in the window. An Excel workbook opens with only 3 worksheets, but you can use 255 per workbook.

Sizing handles

Small squares on the corners and sides of a selected object that can be used for changing its dimensions.

Start

To open an application for use.

Start button

A button on the Taskbar that accesses a special menu that you use to start programs, find files, access Windows Help and more.

Status bar

Displays information regarding your current activity in Excel such as when a cell is ready for editing and when the Number Lock is activated.

Stop Recording toolbar

Toolbar that appears when you are recording a macro. It contains the Stop Recording button and the Relative Reference button.

T

Taskbar

A bar, usually located at the bottom of the screen, that contains the Start button, shows which programs are running by displaying their program buttons, and shows the current time.

Text box

A rectangular area in which text is added so that it can be manipulated independently of the rest of a document.

Title bar

The horizontal bar at the top of a window that displays the name of the document or application that appears in the window.

Toolbar

A graphical bar containing buttons that act as shortcuts for common commands.

V

Values

The numbers, formulas, and functions that Excel uses to perform calculations.

Visual Basic Editor

Allows you to modify a macro using a programming code called Visual Basic.

W

What if analysis

Technique by which you change certain conditions in a worksheet to see how the changes affect the results of your spreadsheet output.

Window

A rectangular area on the screen in which you view and work on files.

Workbook

An Excel file made up of related worksheets. An individual workbook may contain up to 255 worksheets.

Worksheet

The workspace made up of columns and rows where you enter data to create an electronic spreadsheet.

Worksheet tab

The markers near the bottom of the window that identify which worksheet is currently active. To open a different worksheet, click its tab. Worksheet tabs can be named to reflect their contents.

X

X-axis label

A label summarizing the horizontal (x-axis) data on a chart

Y

Y-axis label

A label summarizing the vertical (y-axis) data on a chart.

Index

Notes